Avenues

Teacher's Resource Book

HAMPTON-BROWN

Contents

Masters to Support Language and Literacy Development

Unit 1: Online with Gary Soto 4
Unit 2: Native Land 11
Unit 3: Once Upon a Storm 20
Unit 4: Watery World 29
Unit 5: Cultural Ties 39
Unit 6: This State of Mine 45
Unit 7: What's It Worth? 54
Unit 8: Rocky Tales 61

Writing Project Masters

Write to Give Information: Biography 74
Write to Describe: Description 81
Write to Express Feelings: Personal Narrative 88
Write to Entertain: Story 95

Student Writing Samples

Focus and Coherence 104
Organization 108
Development of Ideas 112
Voice 116

Family Newsletters

in English, Spanish, Vietnamese, Chinese, Korean, Hmong, and Haitian Creole

Unit 1 122
Unit 2 129
Unit 3 136
Unit 4 143
Unit 5 150
Unit 6 157
Unit 7 164
Unit 8 171

Name ______________________ Date ______________

Shoe Sizes

Take off your shoe.
Trace the outline of your foot on the back of the page.
Measure and write the length of the outline.
Find your sizes in columns 2 and 3 of the chart. Then write them.

Inches	U.S. Kids Shoe Sizes	European Kids Shoe Sizes
$7\frac{3}{4}$	$13–13\frac{1}{2}$	31
8	$1–1\frac{1}{2}$	32
$8\frac{1}{4}$	$2–2\frac{1}{2}$	33
$8\frac{1}{2}$	$3–3\frac{1}{2}$	34
9	$4–4\frac{1}{2}$	35
$9\frac{1}{4}$	$5–5\frac{1}{2}$	36

My foot is:

1. __________ inches long.
2. U.S. size __________.
3. European size __________.

If the Shoe Fits

1

Rigo has a big family. He wears used clothes. He wants new clothes. Rigo gets new shoes for his birthday. He puts nickels in his new shoes.

2

A mean boy teases Rigo about his new shoes. Rigo puts the shoes away. He does not wear them for a long time. Then he wants to wear the shoes to a party, but he has grown. The shoes are too small!

3

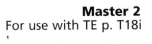

Rigo's uncle has a new job. Rigo gives the shoes to his uncle. His uncle likes the shoes. He gives Rigo two old Mexican coins. Rigo will put them in his next new shoes.

KEY VOCABULARY

Rigo's Journal Entry

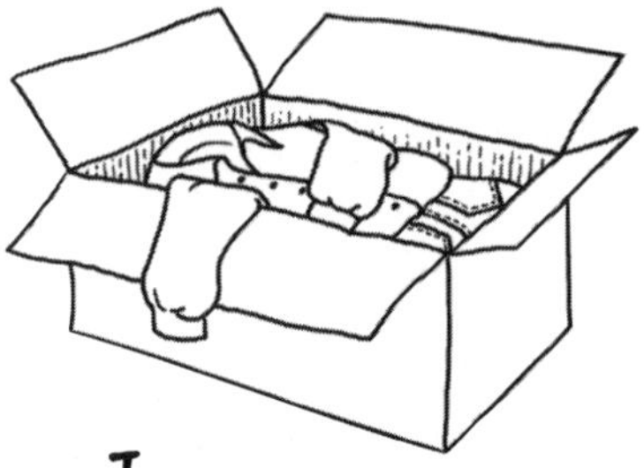

I sure hope I get some **brand-new** clothes for my birthday. I am so tired of **hand-me-down** clothes from my brothers! I don't really **mind** that I am the youngest. What I mind are the horrible **styles** I have to wear! I'm afraid the kids at school will **notice** how I look and laugh at me.

I can't really **refuse** to wear the clothes my brothers have **outgrown**. Mom says I am lucky to have warm clothes and should wear them **proudly**. Sometimes I think Mom just doesn't understand me at all!

Theme Theater Props

Role-Play a Conversation

Use formal language with adults at school and older friends.

Rigo: Mr. Lee, could you help me please?

Mr. Lee: What's the matter, Rigo?

Rigo: Angel was mean to me. He made fun of me. He stole the nickels from my loafers.

Mr. Lee: You must feel scared of Angel.

Rigo: Yes! I'm scared to walk home.

Mr. Lee: Walk home with a friend. Ignore Angel. If he is mean to you again, please tell me.

Use informal language with friends and family.

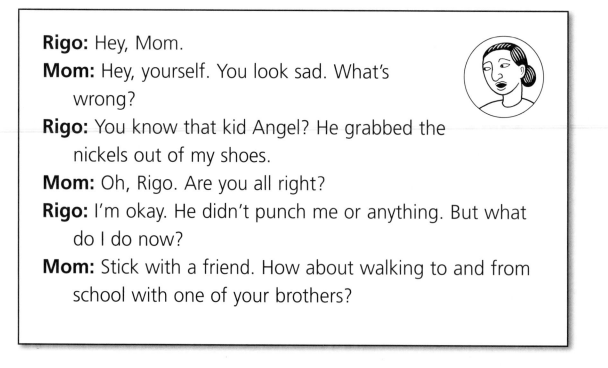

Rigo: Hey, Mom.

Mom: Hey, yourself. You look sad. What's wrong?

Rigo: You know that kid Angel? He grabbed the nickels out of my shoes.

Mom: Oh, Rigo. Are you all right?

Rigo: I'm okay. He didn't punch me or anything. But what do I do now?

Mom: Stick with a friend. How about walking to and from school with one of your brothers?

Name ______________________ Date ____________

Dialogue Journal

What I think:	What do you think?
Page ______	
Page ______	
Page ______	

KEY VOCABULARY

An E-mail About Gary Soto

From... Jesse Singh

To... Kim Nguyen

Subject: Gary Soto

Hey, Kim!

I'm so sorry I didn't **reply** to your message sooner. I've been very busy reading a great story. It's called *If the Shoe Fits*. It is really funny! The kid, Rigo, **reminds** me of myself. He has a big family and some of their **experiences** are just like mine.

I sent an e-mail to the author, Gary Soto, and guess what? He actually answered me! I asked him how he learned to **communicate** so well. He says he uses his **imagination**. Maybe someday I'll write a book, and you can **publish** it for me, okay?

Write back!

How to Make a Dream Catcher

1. Cut a piece of string or yarn four feet long.

2. Tie one end of the string to a ring. Put some beads on the string.

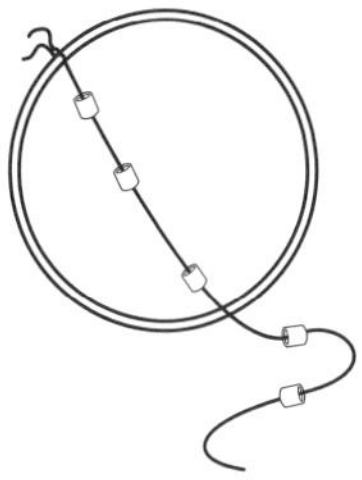

3. Pull the string across the ring. Wrap it around the ring. Add more beads.

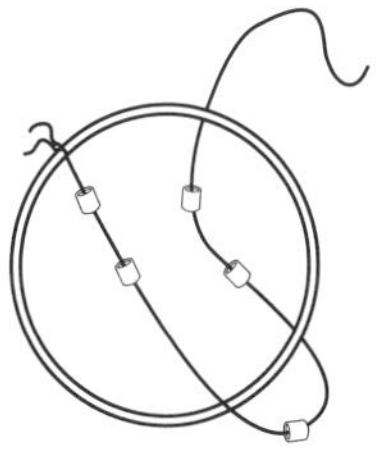

4. Pull the string across the ring again and wrap it around the ring. The string inside the ring should look like two sides of a triangle.

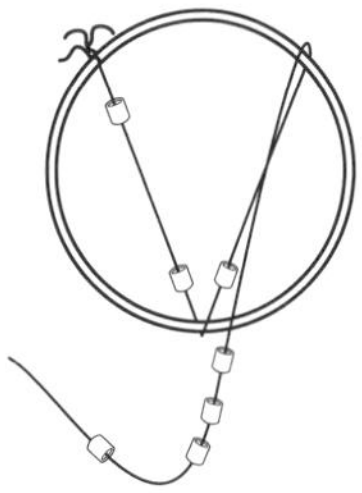

5. Add more beads and wrap the string until you have a web. Tie the end of the string to the ring.

6. Tie feathers or a special object of your own to hang from the bottom.

7. Add a string at the top to hang your dream catcher over your bed.

Name ______________________ Date ______________

Double-Entry Log

Page	What I read	What it reminds me of

Sequel to "Pushing Up the Sky"

Everyone in the **tribe agreed** that the sky was better up high. Children didn't get lost. Grown-ups didn't bump their heads.

But sometimes the sky wanted to be closer to the **village**. It crept down slowly until it was very low. Then everyone got a **pole**. A **chief** gave a loud **signal**. And together the people **pushed up** the sky again.

How a Broomstick Brightened the World

A Story from Sri Lanka
retold by Ann Pilling

The sky was not always as high above the Earth as it is today. Indeed, as the Sun and the Moon traveled around their courses, they often seemed to brush the rooftops, and the stars were so low they were used as lamps outside people's houses.

Once, a servant girl, busy sweeping dust from outside her mistress's house, became very irritated by the passing clouds. They were full of rain, and she kept getting her hair wet. They were also much too low, and they made everything so dim that she could hardly see.

In the end, she lost her temper. "Go away!" she shouted up at the sky. "I can't do anything with you around. You're making my life impossible," and she whacked the sky with her broomstick.

The sky was a creature of great dignity. He did not like being shouted at by a cheeky little servant girl. He gathered his cloudy robes around him and withdrew, floating far, far away until he was well out of reach of the broom. And there he has always remained.

He has no intention of getting thrashed again.

In the East, it is a great insult to hit somebody with a broom. Even wicked demons are scared of them, so it is handy to have one around. No wonder the sky went well out of danger!

KEY POINTS READING

Native Homes

Sturdy Wooden Homes

Some people built wooden homes. Often, many families lived in one large building. These homes kept the families warm and dry.

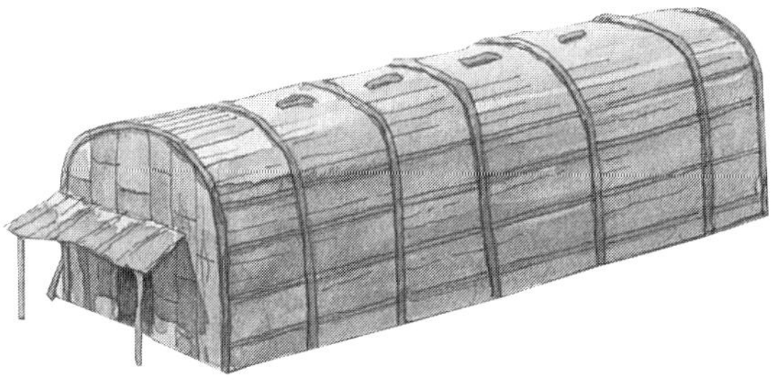

longhouse

plankhouse

Hot Weather Homes

In places where the weather gets very warm, people built homes to keep them cool. It was easy for a cool breeze to blow through these homes.

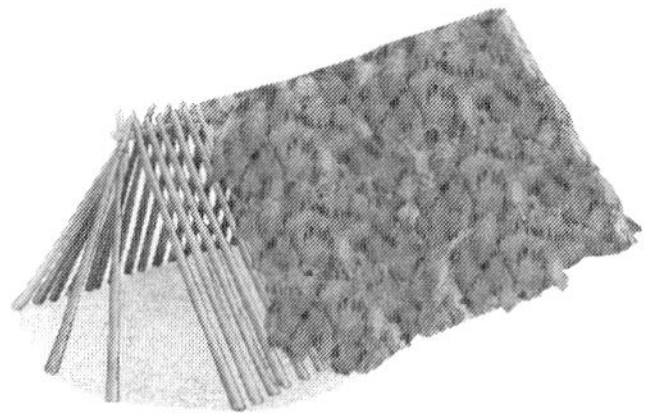

lean-to

woven grass home

wickiup

chickee

Homes That Could Travel

Some Native people moved a lot. They followed the buffalo herds. They needed a home that was easy to carry.

tipi

Homes in the Desert

In the desert Southwest, there are very few trees. People made large homes from mud.

pueblo

Multiple-Meaning Words

bank

(bangk) *noun*

1. The edge of a river or lake is called its **bank**. *Trees grew along the* ***bank*** *of the river.*
2. A **bank** is a place where money is kept. *I put my money in the* ***bank*** *to keep it safe.*

bark

(bark) *noun*

1. When a dog makes a short, loud cry, it is a **bark**. *My dog's* ***bark*** *is very loud.*
2. **Bark** is the outer covering of trees. *Some Native peoples used* ***bark*** *from trees to make their homes.*

sheet

(shēt) *noun*

1. A **sheet** is large, thin cloth used on a bed. *The* ***sheets*** *on my bed are blue.*
2. A large, thin piece of something is called a **sheet**. *They cut dried bark into* ***sheets****.*

trunk

(trungk) *noun*

1. The **trunk** is the main stem of a tree. *People made poles out of tree* ***trunks****.*
2. A **trunk** is a strong box for storing things. *Grandma keeps special clothes in a large* ***trunk****.*
3. An elephant's long nose is called its **trunk**. *The elephant uses its* ***trunk*** *to put food in its mouth.*

Name ______________________ Date ______________

Fluency: Phrasing

Listen to the pauses the reader makes.
Mark short pauses with one line (/).
Mark longer pauses with two lines (//).

Native Homes

Thousands of years before the United States or Canada were countries, hundreds of groups of people lived throughout North America. These were North America's first peoples. They are known as Native peoples, or Native Americans.

In the past, Native people built traditional homes, or lodges, that suited their surroundings, lifestyles, and the climate of the areas in which they lived. Wherever they lived, people always built their homes from natural materials of their region.

In areas of poor soil or little water, Native bands, or groups, had to hunt to survive. These nomadic people followed animal herds and lived in temporary camps. They made shelters of animal hides, grass, tree bark, and fur. These materials were ideal for traveling because they were easy to pack up and move.

KEY VOCABULARY

A Journal Entry About Native Homes

I'm learning a lot about **Native people**. For one thing, they didn't all live in grass houses. They used many different kinds of **materials**. People of some **nations** built houses of mud. Mud houses are **permanent**. Grass houses are **temporary**. In a **region** with lots of trees, people built the **traditional** homes out of leaves over a **frame** of branches.

Tomorrow, I hope we'll learn about foods people ate long ago.

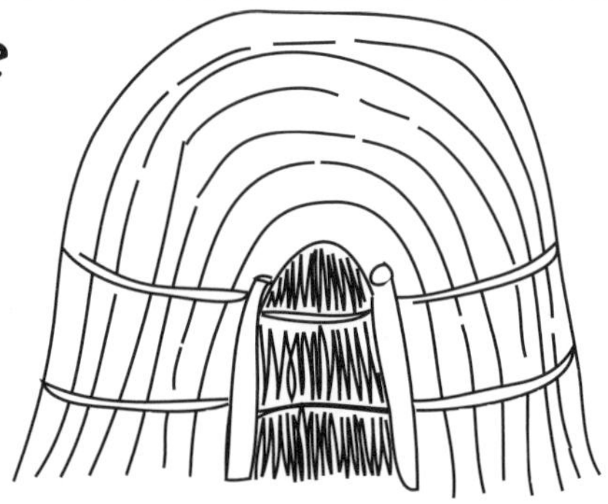

Build a Scale Model

Use this data to build your model home.

Kind of Home	Length	Width	Height
Longhouse 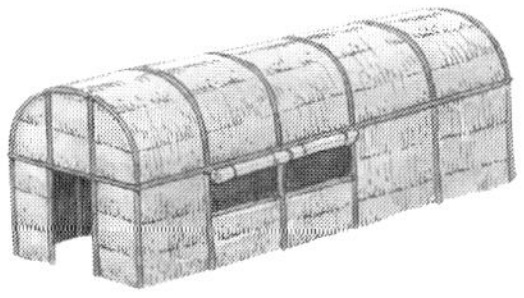	100–200 feet	25 feet	15 feet
Wickiup 	15 feet	15 feet	10 feet
Chickee 	15 feet	10 feet	10 feet
Tipi 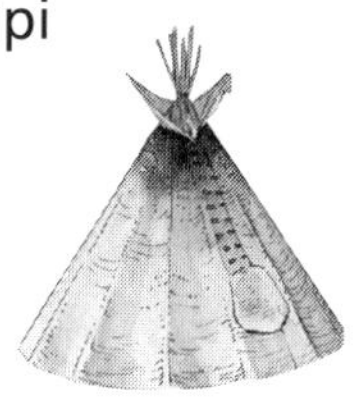	10 feet	10 feet	15 feet
Plankhouse 	50–100 feet	30–60 feet	15 feet

Note that the actual size of homes varied tremendously.
These are rough figures for the purpose of this activity.

Weather Extremes

Temperature Extremes

	Continent	Place	Degrees	Date
Highest Temperatures	Africa	El Azizia, Libya	136 °F	Sept. 13, 1922
	North America	Death Valley, CA	134 °F	July 10, 1913
	Asia	Tirat Tsvi, Israel	129 °F	June 21, 1942
Lowest Temperatures	Antarctica	Vostok	–129 °F	July 21, 1983
	Asia	Oimekon, Russia	–90 °F	Feb. 6, 1933
	Asia	Verkhoyansk, Russia	–90 °F	Feb. 7, 1892

Rainfall Extremes

	Continent	Place	Average Rainfall
Highest Annual Rainfall	South America	Lloro, Columbia	$523\frac{1}{2}$ inches
	Asia	Mawsynram, India	$467\frac{1}{2}$ inches
	Oceania	Mt. Waialeale, Hawaii	460 inches
Lowest Annual Rainfall	South America	Arica, Chile	less than $\frac{1}{30}$ of an inch
	Asia	Wadi Halfa, Sudan	less than $\frac{1}{10}$ of an inch
	Antarctica	South Pole Station	$\frac{4}{5}$ of an inch

KEY POINTS READING

Twister

Lucille and Natt play outside. They see a storm coming. They go inside. It's a twister! Lucille and Natt run to the cellar. They will be safe there. Mom goes to help their neighbor, Mr. Lyle.

The cellar is dark. Lucille and Natt are scared. They play games. They hear a loud roar. Lucille and Natt hold the chain to keep the cellar door shut. The twister passes.

Mama has not come back. Is she safe? Lucille and Natt leave the cellar. They see Mama and Mr. Lyle! The storm is over. Everyone is safe.

A Letter to Lucille and Natt

Dear Lucille and Natt,

That **twister** must have been scary. I've never seen one, but we do have **thunder** and **lightning** and **hail** sometimes.

Our neighbor's dog Nicky doesn't like thunder. Sometimes during a storm, we can hear his **howling**. Once, he was so scared, he broke into our **cellar**. Dad went down to get some canned peaches, and there was Nicky, **silent** as a mouse. I took him home and then helped Mom fix the **damage** to the cellar door.

Your friend,

Gina

Name ______________________ Date ____________

KWLQ Chart

K What I know	W What I want to learn	L What I learned	Q Questions I still have

Weather Reports

Listen to this weather report.

Hello and welcome to Weather Watch. The forecast for tomorrow is for fair weather with temperatures in the upper 70s. Winds are from the northwest at 12 miles per hour. A cold front from Canada could bring showers tomorrow night.

First, read this weather forecast with an informal tone.
Then read it with a formal tone.

Good morning. This is Weather World. Today's weather will be sunny all day. The high temperature will be 75. Tonight will be cooler. Look for clouds tomorrow morning and rain tomorrow afternoon.

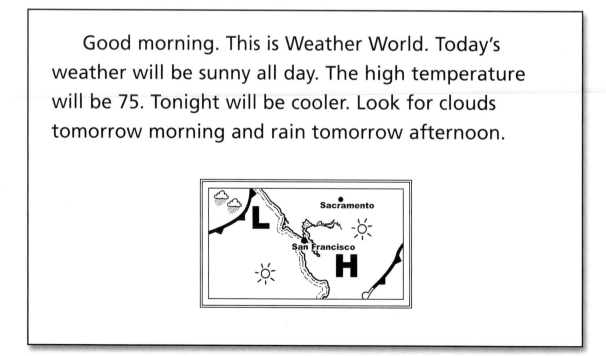

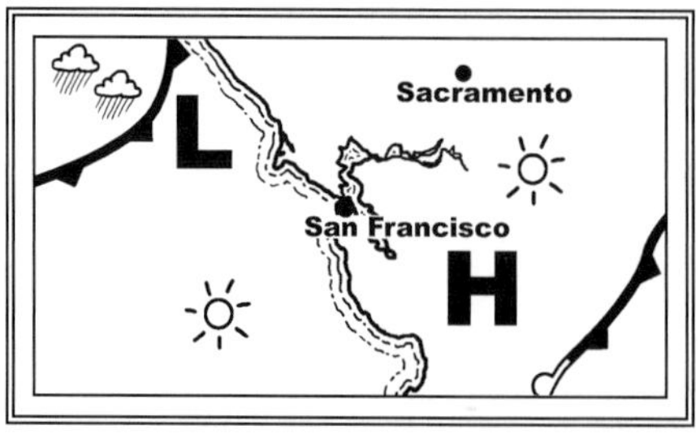

Name ____________________ Date ____________

Fluency: Phrasing

Listen to the pauses the reader makes.
Mark short pauses with one line (/).
Mark longer pauses with two lines (//).

The Big Storm

It was a beautiful spring morning across most of the United States on the last day of March in 1982. Spring is a time of rapidly changing weather.

In the west, a mass of clouds and cold, damp air rolled in off the ocean. It was the start of the big storm.

The clouds brought heavy rain to the Pacific Coast as the storm moved inland. It was carried along by the winds that nearly always blow from west to east across the continent.

Soon the storm ran up against the mountains of the Sierra Nevada range in California. The wind pushed the clouds up the steep slopes. In the cold mountain air, the rain changed to snow.

KEY VOCABULARY

A Letter to Bruce Hiscock

Dear Mr. Hiscock,

I liked your article. I want to be a weather **forecaster**. I like storms even though they can be **dangerous**.

We had a **blizzard** last winter. A **cold front** pushed a big **mass** of cold air into our area. The **temperature** was about 15 degrees. We had 37 inches of snow!

In the summer we have **thunderstorms**. One year we even had a **tornado**!

Thank you for writing such an interesting article.

Sincerely,

Yuko

Name ______________________ Date ______________

Storm Tally Sheet

List different storms. Survey five people.
Place a check mark (✔) for each storm they have seen.
Total the check marks for each row.

Kind of Storm	People Who Have Seen This Kind of Storm	Total

Glossary for "The Big Storm"

barometer (bu-**rom**-u-tur) *noun* [Gk *baros* weight + *metron* measure] A **barometer** is an instrument that measures air pressure in the atmosphere. It tells if the air pressure is high or low. *The **barometer** showed that air pressure was low this morning.*

beautiful (**byū**-ti-ful) *adjective* Something **beautiful** is pleasing to look at or hear. From **beauty**. *We loved listening to the **beautiful** music.*

blizzard (**bliz**-urd) *noun* A **blizzard** is a heavy snowstorm with strong, cold winds. *Wind blew the snow around during the **blizzard**.*

climate (**klī**-mut) *noun* **Climate** is the usual weather in a place. *The **climate** in the desert is hot and dry.*

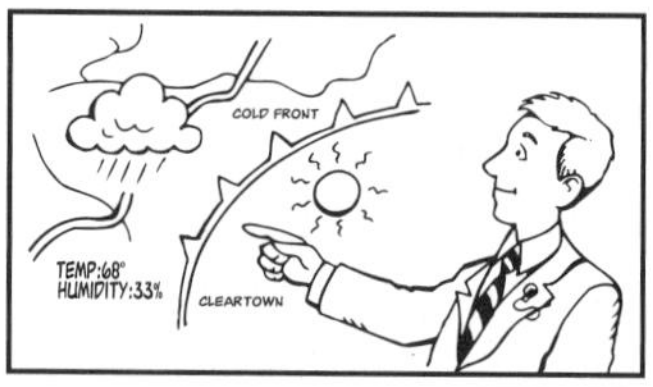

forecaster (**for**-kast-ur) *noun* [OE *fore* before + ME *cast* ti throw + ME *er* one who] A **forecaster** predicts the weather. From **forecast**. *The **forecaster** says it will rain tomorrow.*

humid (**hyū**-mud) *adjective* When it is **humid**, the air feels wet. ***Humid** air makes my skin feel sticky.*

inland (**in**-lund) *adjective* An **inland** place is away from the coast. *The storm moved **inland** toward the mountains.*

Ocean Facts

Use these facts to compare the oceans of the world.

Ocean Name	Area in Square Miles	Average Depth in Feet	Greatest Depth in Feet
Pacific Ocean	60,667,230	13,215	35,831
Atlantic Ocean	29,937,180	12,880	28,224
Indian Ocean	26,736,840	13,002	23,806
Southern Ocean	7,927,530	13,100–16,400	23,731
Arctic Ocean	5,481,840	3,953	15,301

The Secret Footprints

1

Ciguapas live underwater. Their feet are on backward. This keeps people from finding them. One night, a boy sees Guapa, and she runs away. The ciguapa queen is angry. She says that people are not nice. Guapa makes a promise. She will stay away from people.

2

Later, Guapa sees the boy's family having a picnic. She forgets her promise. When the family goes for a walk, Guapa eats their cakes. The family finds her, so Guapa pretends to be hurt. The family goes to get a doctor, but the boy stays with Guapa.

3

The boy is very kind. When he goes to get water for Guapa, she runs away. She leaves a seashell for him. Guapa tells the queen that the boy is nice. The queen lets Guapa go near the people's house. Sometimes the boy looks for Guapa. He always leaves cakes for her.

KEY VOCABULARY

A Letter to Guapa

Dear **secret** friend,

I'm sorry you ran away after the picnic. I couldn't find your footprints. It was very **mysterious**. Then one night I saw you outside. I saw your **backward** feet. That's when I **discovered** how you hide so well.

I am **curious** about you and want to be your friend. I like your **boldness**. Please come again. And please don't worry. Humans will not **capture** you. I **promise** no one will ever hurt you.

Your friend,

the boy

Scene 3: The Woods

Guapa lies on the blanket. The family stands over her, concerned.

Narrator: The family thinks Guapa's feet are badly hurt, and they go for a doctor. The boy stays. Guapa knows the ciguapas are near.

The family leaves the stage. Ciguapas whisper and hoot softly offstage.

Boy: What can I get you? (*He offers Guapa* a pastelito.)

Guapa: I would like some water.

The boy leaves to get water. The ciguapas rush onstage and help Guapa walk offstage. Guapa leaves a seashell for the boy. The boy returns with a glass of water and looks at the shell with a puzzled expression.

Narrator: The ciguapas learn that humans can be kind. The boy keeps the shell to remember his mysterious friend. Sometimes Guapa folds the family's clothes. She finds *pastelitos* the boy leaves in his pockets.

The boy stands on one side of the stage, holding the shell. Guapa stands on the other side. She holds a pair of the boy's pants and is pulling a pastelito *out of the pocket.*

Theme Theater

The Secret Footprints

Setting

Scene 1: In the Ciguapas' Cave and Outside the Boy's Home

Scene 2: The Woods

Scene 3: The Woods

Cast of Characters

Narrators	Guapa
Queen	Boy
Other ciguapas	Other humans

Scene 1: In the Ciguapas' Cave and Outside the Boy's Home

The boy is offstage behind his house. Guapa, the queen, and other ciguapas are onstage.

Narrator: The ciguapas live underwater. They have a secret that keeps them safe from humans: their feet are on backward. One ciguapa, Guapa, is very curious about life on land.

Guapa walks toward the boy's home.

Narrator: One night Guapa goes near a house.

Guapa *(tries on clothes)*: This one fits me!

Boy (*shouts out window*): *¡Hola!*

Guapa runs back to the cave.

Narrator: The tribe is worried Guapa will be caught. They ask the queen to speak to Guapa.

Ciguapas whisper worriedly.

Queen *(angrily)*: Stop being such a mischief!

Guapa: I'm bold and curious about everything. That's why you named me Guapa.

Queen: You must stop taking chances! Humans are not nice!

Guapa *(hangs her head)*: I promise.

Scene 2: The Woods

The family is eating a picnic lunch.

Narrator: Guapa keeps her promise, but one afternoon she forgets and goes into the woods.

Guapa *(comes on stage)*: It's a beautiful day. Maybe the boy is out playing.

Guapa sees the family and watches them. They eat and talk quietly, but they do not see Guapa.

Boy: Let's take a walk.

The boy and his family walk away.

Guapa: I am so hungry. Their food looks good. I'll eat some while they're gone. *(sneaks over and takes some food)*

The boy and his family return and see Guapa. She tries to leave, but she falls.

Amazing Facts

That's Amazing!

An amazing fact about ______________________________

is ______________________________

____

I found it in the book ______________________________

by ______________________________

______________________________ Name

______________________________ Date

That's Amazing!

An amazing fact about ______________________________

is ______________________________

____

I found it in the book ______________________________

by ______________________________

______________________________ Name

______________________________ Date

Name ____________________ Date ____________________

Fluency: Phrasing

Listen to the pauses the reader makes.
Mark short pauses with one line (/).
Mark longer pauses with two lines (//).

Hello, Fish!

Actually, all frogs, fish, birds, mammals, turtles, lizards, and snakes have something in common. We all have backbones, called vertebrae, unlike most of the rest of life on Earth. Beetles don't, crabs don't, starfish don't, octopuses don't, nor do jellyfish, of course! Those who have backbones are frogs and fish and people everywhere, including you!

Seahorses are small fish with large eyes. They have a big appetite for tiny crustaceans. Like people, they choose partners for life. They usually stay together, even during stormy weather.

Seahorse mothers lay their eggs in special pouches that seahorse fathers have in their bellies. Weeks later, fully formed little fish swim out of the pouches into the sea. They are ready to grow up and find partners of their own.

KEY VOCABULARY

A Letter to Wolcott Henry

Dear Mr. Henry,

I love your underwater photographs of ocean **creatures**! The fish really **blend** into their backgrounds. **Camouflage** is a great **defense**. It saves the fish from **deadly** enemies. My favorite photo is of the stargazer. I can hardly see it in the sand!

I like how the brown goby finds **safety**, too. That worm tube is a good **shelter**.

All your photos are great!

Your fan,

Juanita

P.S. It was interesting to learn that all these fish have **backbones**. I didn't know that.

Make a Food Chain

Look at this food chain. It shows that a boy eats beef from a cow and the cow eats grass.

boy

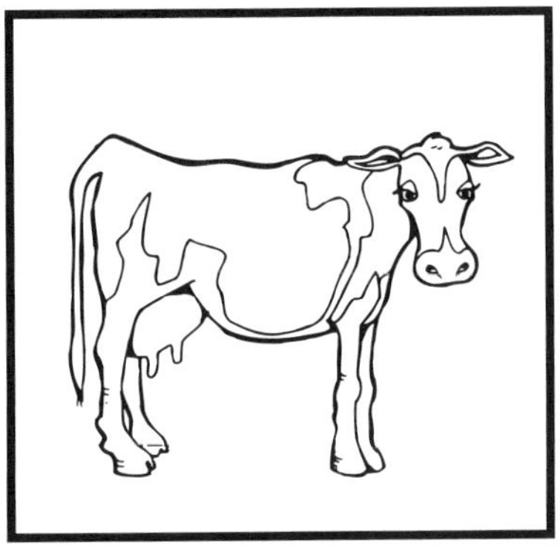

beef

grass

Now use this information to make your food chain.

What People Eat	Where the Food Comes From
beef, steak, hamburger, bologna	cow
pork, hot dogs, pork chops, bacon, ham	pig
apple	apple tree
pasta, bread	wheat plant
chicken	chicken
tortilla	corn plant, wheat plant
rice	rice plant
potatoes	potato plant
peanut	peanut plant

Animal	What It Eats
cow	grass, hay, corn
pig	milk, corn
chicken	corn, grass, soybeans, worms
worm	things in the soil

Name ______________________ Date ____________

Aquarium Tour Evaluation

Use this form to record details and your opinions about the aquarium tours.

Aquarium Name and Location	Exhibits	What I Liked	What I Didn't Like	How I Feel About this Aquarium

World Market Price List

Here are the prices of items you might find at a world market.

Decorations

Item	Country	Price
lacquered box	Japan	$1.99 each
toss pillow	India	$9.99 for two
ceramic vase	Vietnam	$15.99 each
wooden mirror	China	$19.99 each

Toys

Item	Country	Price
wooden puzzle	Germany	$5.99 each
bead craft kit	United States	$10.99 each
animal trivia game	England	$12.99 each
dragon kite	Indonesia	$19.99 each

Foods

Item	Country	Price
biscotti cookies	Italy	$2.99 per box
salsa	Mexico	$5.99 for two jars
all-fruit jam	England	$3.99 per jar
coffee	Kenya	$9.99 per pound

KEY POINTS READING

The Lotus Seed

1

Bà lives in Vietnam. The emperor of Vietnam loses his job and cries. Bà takes a lotus seed from his garden. She wants to remember this day. Bà hides the seed.

2

Then there is a war. Bà and her family leave Vietnam. They go to a strange, new country. She takes the lotus seed with her.

3

Many years later, Bà's grandson takes the seed. He forgets where he plants it. Bà cries.

4

Then a pink lotus flower blooms in the spring. Bà is very happy. The lotus flower is the special flower of Vietnam. Bà gives each grandchild a seed from the lotus, and she keeps one for herself.

KEY VOCABULARY

Sequel to "The Lotus Seed"

Bà's granddaughter, Anh, grew up and had a son. One day, her son found her **lotus** seed in a **special** jar. Anh almost **forgot** it was there.

Anh told her son Bà's story: how she was sad when the **emperor** lost his **throne** and how Bà left her country and **arrived** in the United States.

"Let's plant the seed to help us **remember** Bà," Anh said quietly.

The next spring, they saw a beautiful pink lotus **bloom**. Anh carefully kept its seeds, but only after she gave one to her son.

Name ________________________ Date ____________

Reflection Journal

Page	My question	The answer

A Letter from the U.S.

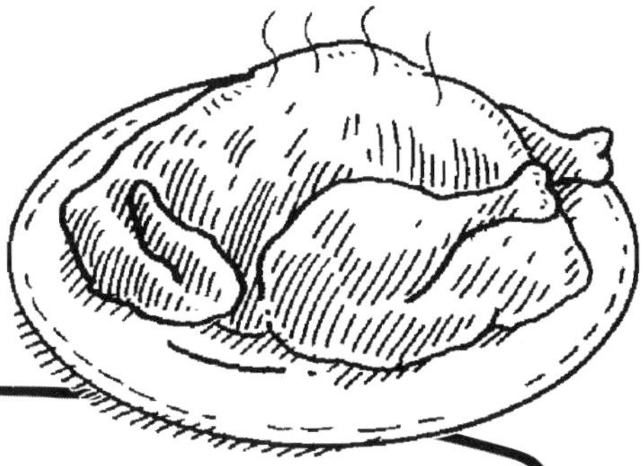

Dear Cousin Marta,

It is wonderful to live in the United States, but it is hard to **adjust** to life in a new country. Father says we came here for a **better future,** but things are so different from where we **come from.**

Here we celebrate new holidays like Thanksgiving. I didn't like the turkey!

Papa reminds me that the United States is the land of **opportunity.** We can live here and feel **pride** in both our **cultures.**

I hope you can visit soon. I miss you!

Your cousin,

Jorge

Name ______________________ Date ____________

An Interview with ______________________

Write your interview questions. List follow-up questions you can ask, too.
Then write the answer to each question.
Add any other information you need for your introduction.

My questions:	The answers:
Follow-up questions:	

Name ______________________ Date ______________

Sensory Observations

Name a place in your community. Write or draw to tell what you can see, hear, smell, touch, and taste there. Some spaces will be blank.

Place: ______________________

	Plants	Animals	Landforms	Foods
What I See				
What I Hear				
What I Smell				
What I Touch				
What I Taste				

Word Detective

New Word: ______________________________

What I think it means: ______________________________

____

Clues: ______________________________

____

Definition: ______________________________

____

______________________________ Name ______________ Date

New Word: ______________________________

What I think it means: ______________________________

____

Clues: ______________________________

____

Definition: ______________________________

____

______________________________ Name ______________ Date

Name ______________________ Date ____________

Fluency: Phrasing and Accuracy

Listen to the pauses the reader makes.
Mark short pauses with one line (/).
Mark longer pauses with two lines (//).

A Quarter's Worth of Fame

Mr. Stanley: So you drew a minuteman soldier.

Xander: Not at first. I started with the easiest part of my idea. I drew the outline of the state. Then, on the right side, I drew the *Mayflower*. That's the ship that people used to get from England to Massachusetts in 1620.

Mr. Stanley: That sounds like a pretty complicated sketch. It must have been difficult to draw.

Xander: It was terrible. I erased it and drew it again. On the left side, I drew a smiling minuteman.

Mr. Stanley: Let me guess: It was terrible, and you drew it again.

Scoring Chart

Total Words Read in One Minute	Minus Words Missed	Total Words Read Correctly

KEY VOCABULARY

A Journal Entry with an Idea

When I read about Xander, I thought that our school should have a **contest**. Students could make a poster **design** for their class. Students who want to enter can make a **sketch** of how to **honor** their class.

My friend Jenna can draw well. She has **talent**. Maybe we could work together. I'd like our poster to show a circle of kids holding hands. That would show how we are all very good friends.

Name ______________________ Date ______________

Quarter Data Chart

Make a mark in the Tally column for each quarter you see.
Add the marks and write the totals in the Total column and the bottom row.
Calculate and write the percentages in the % column.
The percentage total should equal 100%.

	Tally	Total	%
State Quarters			
Other Quarters			
Grand Total			100%

KEY POINTS READING

The Tree That Would Not Die

1

An acorn falls to the ground. It grows into an oak tree. The First People meet under the tree. Spanish soldiers come. They call the land "Tejas." The First People sit under the tree with Stephen F. Austin. They sign a peace treaty. Now the tree is called the Treaty Oak.

2

The tree keeps growing. Many settlers come. Texas becomes a new country. The land around the tree is the capital. It is called Austin. Then Texas becomes part of the United States. Houses crowd the tree. People want to cut it down.

3

Children want to save the tree. They send money, and the city builds a park around the tree. Then a man poisons the tree. Many people work hard, and they save the tree. The Treaty Oak is still growing today.

Glossary of Social Studies Words

boundary (**bown**-du-rē) *noun* A separating line between two places.

capital (**kap**-ut-l) *noun* Where the center of a government is located.

government (**guv**-urn-munt) *noun* The organization that rules or controls a country or town; from the root word **govern**.

Word History

The word *govern* comes from several languages including Old French *governer*; from Greek *kybernan*; from Latin *gubernare,* to steer.

Related Words: govern, governor

settlement (**set**-l-munt) *noun* A group of homes in one area; from the root word **settle**.

Word History

The word *settle* comes from Old English *setl* seat, place of rest.

Related Words: settle, settler

settler (**set**-lur) *noun* A person who builds a home in a new area.

treaty (**trēt**-ē) *noun* An agreement.

Pronunciation Key

ā	cake
ē	key
ī	bike
ō	goat
ū	fruit
yū	mule

KEY VOCABULARY

A Letter to the Treaty Oak

Dear Treaty Oak,

My class read a story about how the land around you became the **capital** of Texas. We learned that the First People signed a **treaty** with Stephen Austin under your branches to promise **peace** with each other. That's how you got your name! You were the **boundary** between the First People's land and the **settlements** Stephen Austin's people built.

Now our state **government** is there. And next week we're coming to visit you. I can't wait to meet you!

Your friend,
Camilla

Name ______________________ Date ______________

Estimate Tree Height: Method A

1. First, measure and write your partner's height. ________

2. Have your partner stand next to the tree while you stand farther away, in front of the tree.

3. Then, hold up a ruler. Align the top of it with the top of your partner's head.

4. Next, place your finger on the ruler to mark where you see your partner's feet.

5. Now, measure the tree by holding up the ruler and counting how many times the marked area goes into the tree's height. Write the number. ________

6. Finally, multiply your partner's height by this number. Write the answer. This is the height of the tree. ________

Name ______________________ Date ______________

Estimate Tree Height: Method B

1. Measure the length of your partner's shadow and write it. ________

2. Measure your partner's height and write it. ________

3. Measure the length of the tree's shadow and write it. ________

4. Multiply the answer to Step 3 by the answer to Step 2 and write the answer. ________

5. Divide the answer to Step 4 by the answer to Step 1 and write it. This is the height of the tree. ________

Name ______________________ Date ______________

Balance a Checkbook

How to Write a Check

1. Write the date.
2. Write who the money is paid to.
3. Write the amount in figures ($5.00).
4. Write the amount in words (five and 00/100).
5. Sign your name.

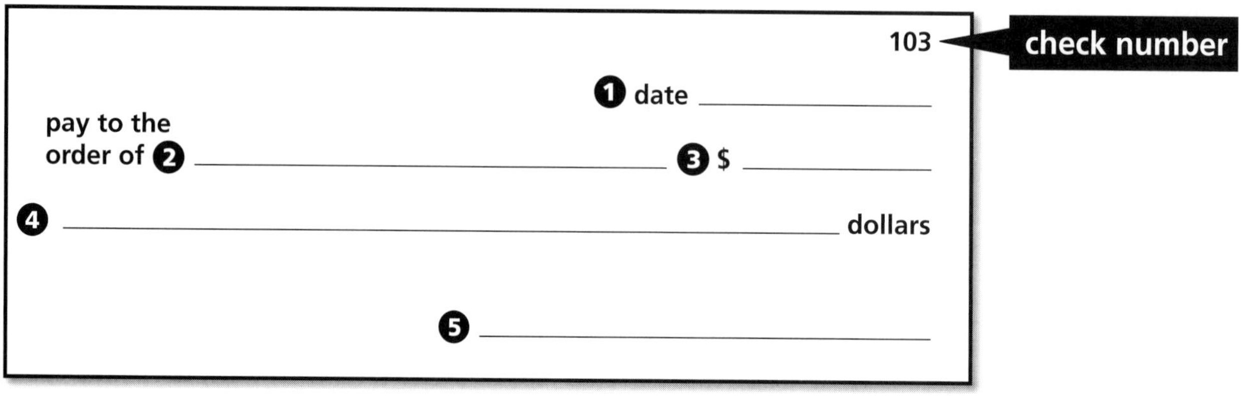

How to Balance a Checkbook

1. Write the check number in column 1 and the date in column 2.
2. In column 3, write the name of the person or business you wrote the check to.
3. In column 4, write the amount of the check.
4. Subtract the amount of the check from the last balance and write the new balance in column 5.

Number	Date	Paid To	Amount	Balance
100	Jan. 3	Meg's Pet Care	$15.00	$75.00
101	Jan. 5	Let's Go Sports	$12.75	$62.25
102	Jan. 10	Town Flower Shop	$9.00	$53.25

Name ______________________________ Date ______________

Prediction Chart

What I know about the character	What I think will happen

KEY VOCABULARY

A Letter from Saruni

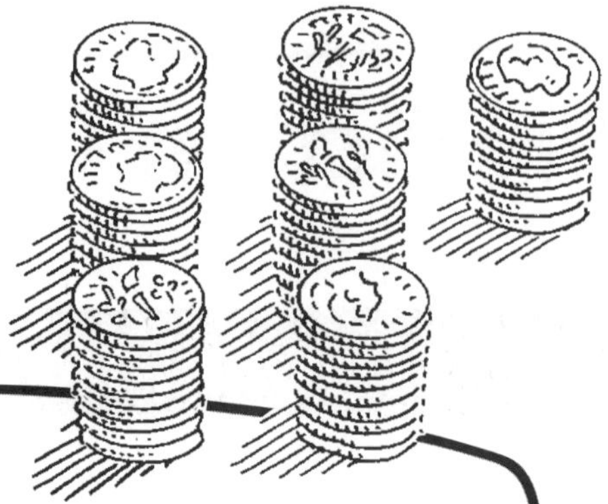

Dear Yeyo and Murete,

Thank you very much for the bicycle and for my box of **coins**! You knew I was **disappointed** when I couldn't buy a bike. I looked around the **market** at the other **goods**. There was nothing else I really wanted. I was **determined** to get the bike. I wanted it to carry **loads** for Yeyo.

It was a big surprise when Murete sold the bike to me. It was an even bigger surprise when Yeyo returned my money as a **reward**! Thank you so much!

Love,
Saruni

Name ______________________________ Date ______________

My Budget

My Weekly Budget

Money In

______________________________ $ __________

______________________________ $ __________

______________________________ $ __________

Total Money In: $ __________

Money Out

______________________________ $ __________

______________________________ $ __________

______________________________ $ __________

Total Money Out: $ __________

Subtract Total Money Out from Total Money In.
This is how much I can save each week. **$** __________

What I want: ______________________________

What it costs: $ __________

When I divide what it costs by how much I can save each week, I get: ________ weeks.
This is how long I have to save.

KEY POINTS READING

Money

MONEY

What does it mean?

something of value; something people use to trade for things they want

How is it used?

If you trade a blanket for food, the blanket is like money.

You can pay for a shirt with dollars. You can trade lunches with a friend. The dollars and the lunches are both kinds of money.

You can exchange one country's money for another country's money.

What is it like?

Shells, tea, and salt are kinds of money used long ago.

Money is made of metal and paper. Coins are metal money. They are made of zinc, copper, and nickel. All money has a special design on it.

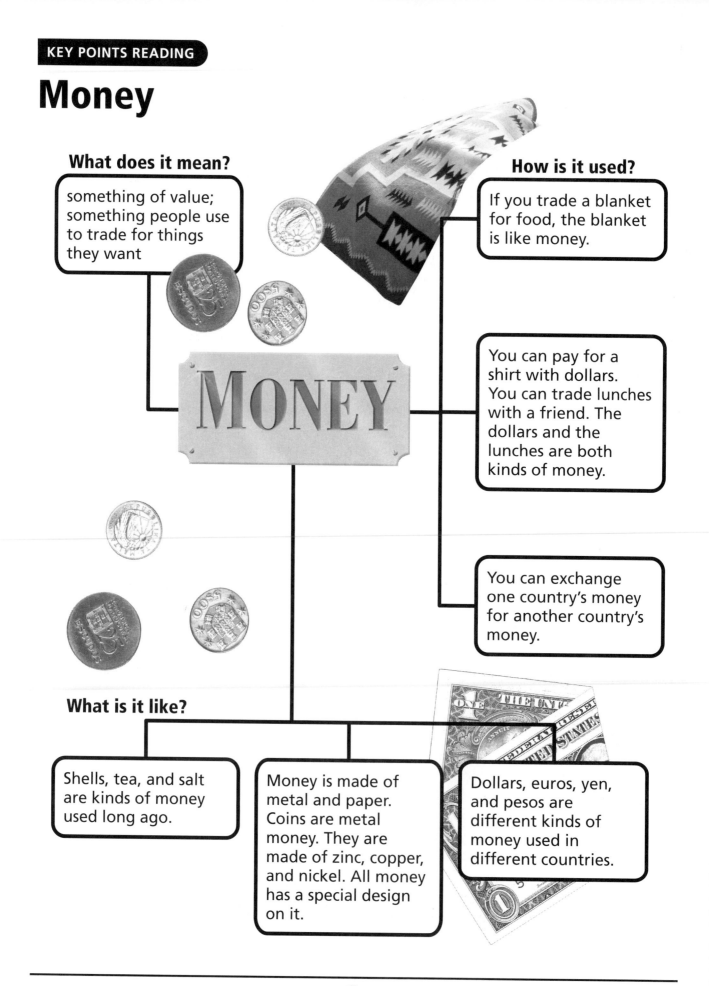

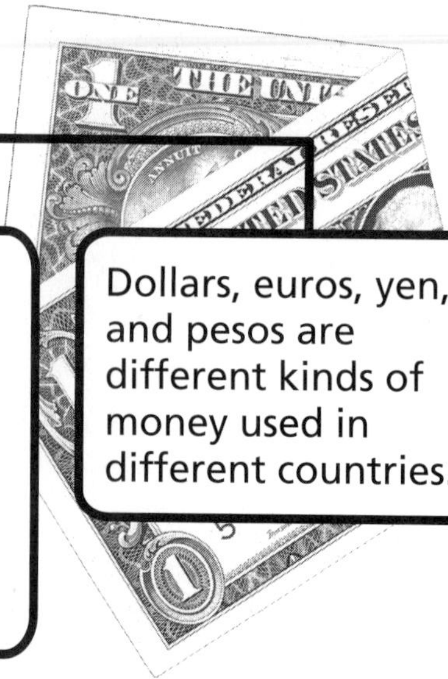

Dollars, euros, yen, and pesos are different kinds of money used in different countries.

KEY VOCABULARY

A Journal Entry About Money

We learned a lot about money today. There are different kinds of money all over the world. It has different **values** in different places.

Once there wasn't any money. Everyone **bartered** or **traded services**. I guess it's like my mom and Mr. Gomez. They **exchange** help. Mom helped Mr. Gomez build a porch. Mr. Gomez helped Mom fix our car. It's so interesting to learn about something we use every day.

Name ______________________ Date ____________

Which Costs More?

To compare the prices of products, calculate the price per unit of measure.

To calculate the price per ounce, use this equation:
price ÷ total number of ounces = price per ounce

Susie's Sugar: \$.99 ÷ 16 = \$.06
Sam's Sugar: \$1.69 ÷ 32 = \$.05

Which sugar has the lower price per ounce? ____________

Susie's Sugar
Amount: 16 ounces
Price: \$.99

Sam's Sugar
Amount: 32 ounces
Price: \$1.69

Practice with this example:

To calculate the price per egg, use this equation:
price ÷ total number of eggs = price per egg

Elsa's Eggs: \$1.79 ÷ 12 = \$____________
Ernie's Eggs: \$1.19 ÷ 6 = \$____________

Which eggs have the lower price per egg? ____________

Elsa's Eggs
Amount: 12 eggs
Price: \$1.79

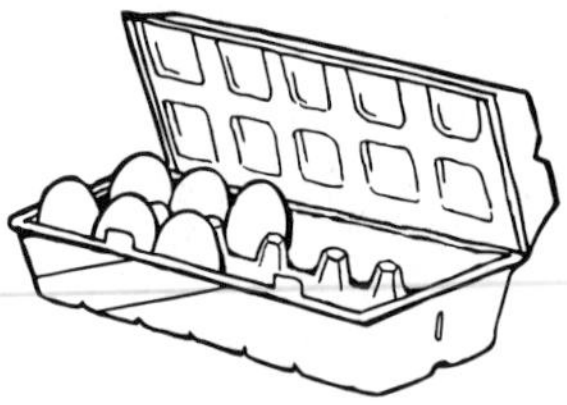

Ernie's Eggs
Amount: 6 eggs
Price \$1.19

Now compare the prices per unit of products in the class store.

Product	Price	÷ Total Units of Measure	= Price Per Unit of Measure
		÷	=
		÷	=
		÷	=
		÷	=
		÷	=

Name ______________________ Date ______________

A Lifetime of Rock

Here are the amounts of rocks, minerals, and metals that one person in the U.S. uses during a lifetime.

Rock, Mineral, or Metal	Amount in Pounds
bauxite (aluminum)	5,691
cement	67,826
coal	590,746
copper	1,615
clay	20,763

Rock, Mineral, or Metal	Amount in Pounds
iron ore	42,141
lead	1,000
salt	32,221
stone, sand, gravel	1,650,000
zinc	923

Find the amounts of several kinds of rocks your family will use in a lifetime.

1. In column 1, write the name of the rock.
2. In column 2, write the amount of that kind of rock that one person uses in a year.
3. In column 4, write the number of people in your family.
4. Multiply the amount of rock times the number of people in your family.
5. Write the total in column 6.

Name of Rock	Amount of Rock	×	Number of People	=	Total Amount
		×		=	
		×		=	
		×		=	
		×		=	

KEY POINTS READING

Call Me Ahnighito

1

Ahnighito is a meteorite that fell from space to Earth. He landed in the snow in Greenland. He sits in the snow for hundreds of years. Finally something happens! People find him and take little pieces of him. Ahnighito is not happy.

2

Hundreds of years later, other people try to put him onto a ship. The weather gets too cold, and the people sail away. People return but have to leave again. Finally, new people come and get him onto a ship. A little girl names him Ahnighito. Ahnighito is excited!

3

The ship sails to the big city of New York, but Ahnighito has to sit outside on the dock. He is bored. After seven years, people move him to a new home in a museum. Many people visit him every day. Ahnighito is not lonely anymore.

A Letter to Ahnighito

Dear Ahnighito,

You are an **enormous meteorite**! No wonder people had to **strain** so hard to **lift** you. They really wanted to take you on the long **journey** to the **museum**.

You must have felt so **lonely** when the people **abandoned** you in Greenland.

Now I think you are happy in the museum.

Here is how I feel about visiting you!

Your fan,
Shakira

Map of New York City

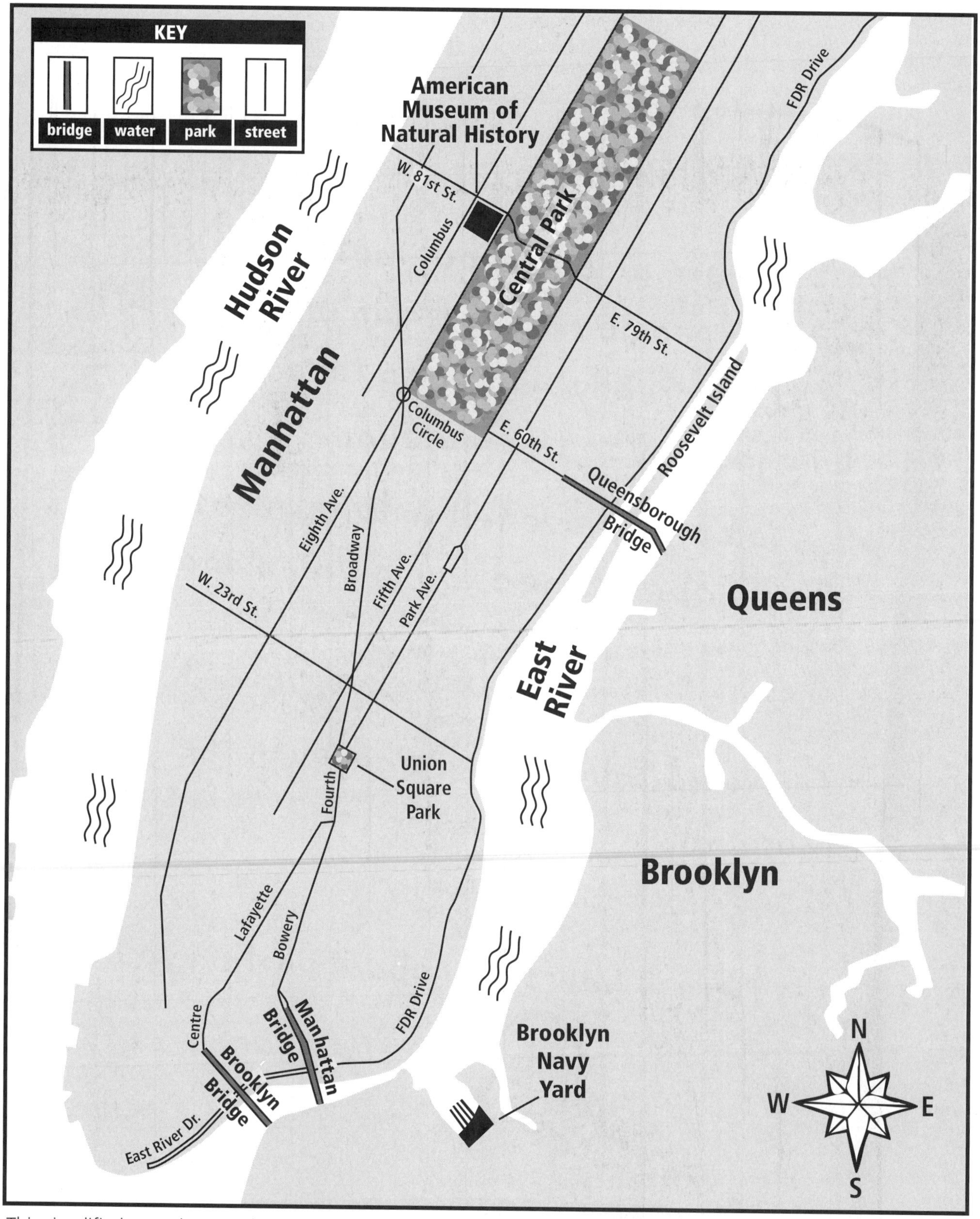

This simplified map shows only major streets for the purpose of this activity.

Interpret Charts and Diagrams

Meteorite Fact Chart				
Meteorite	**Where It Came From**	**Where It Landed**	**When It Was Found**	**Mass (grams)**
NWA 1195	Mars	Morocco	March 2002	315
NWA 1068	Mars	Western Sahara	April 2001	578
Y000593	Mars	Antarctica	November 2000	13,700
Dhofar 019	Mars	Oman	January 2000	1,056
NWA 773	Moon	Western Sahara	September 2000	633
Dhofar 287	Moon	Oman	January 2001	154

Meteorite Hitting the Earth

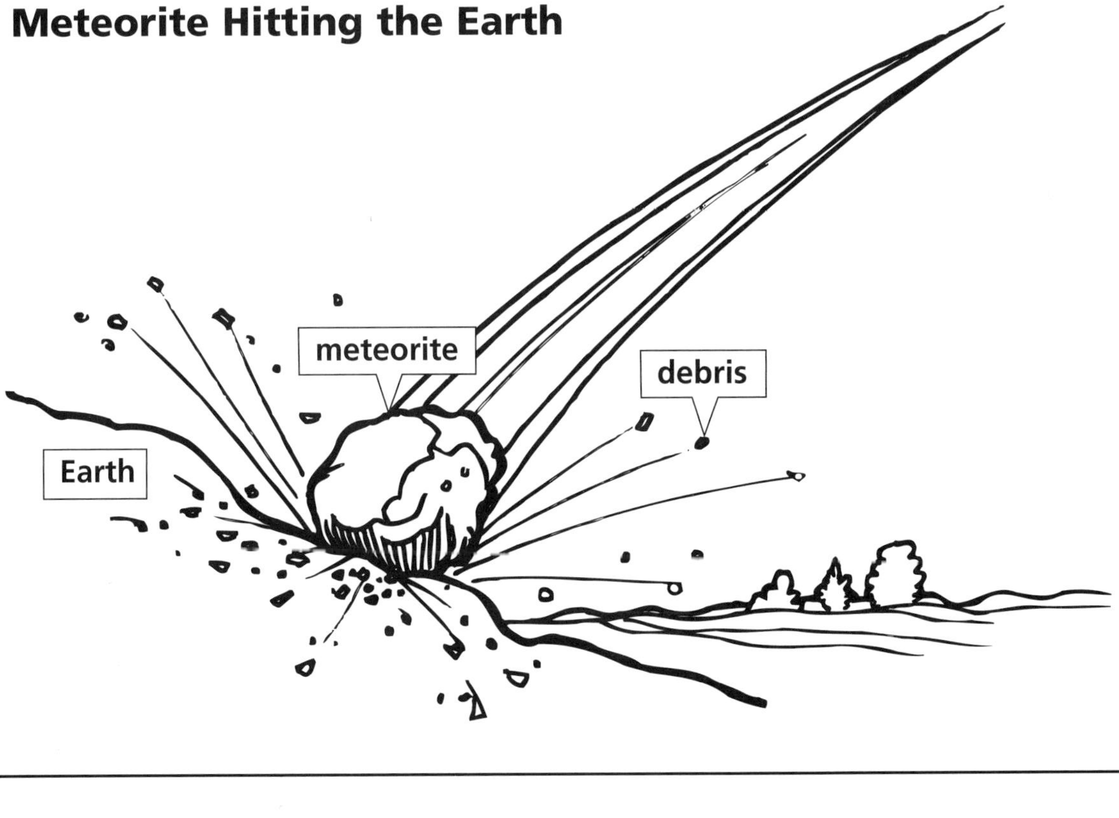

Name ______________________ Date ______________

Strategy Planner

Step 1 What is the author's purpose for writing?

☐ to tell a story

☐ to entertain

OR

☐ to give information

Step 2 What is your purpose for reading?

☐ for enjoyment **OR** ☐ for information

Step 3 What type of story are you going to read?

☐ **fiction** **OR** ☐ **nonfiction**

Do the following:

- Identify the characters and settings.
- Think about what happens and when it happens.
- Use what you know to read new words.

Do the following:

- Read (more) slowly.
- Identify facts about real people or events.
- Use maps, diagrams, and pictures.
- Concentrate as you read.

Name ______________________ Date ____________

Fluency: Phrasing and Accuracy

Listen to the pauses the reader makes.
Mark short pauses with one line (/).
Mark longer pauses with two lines (//).

The Life Story of a Rock

Day to day, rocks are useful in our world. Rock caves provide shelter for animals that need places to hide or rest. On a windy day, underground rocks give trees a place to hold on tight.

People use rocks in all kinds of construction. Rocks help make concrete for sidewalks, highways, and skyscrapers. Rocks can make a strong wall. Thin pieces of rock can make a pretty floor in a house.

Rocks are also important for plant growth. In the topsoil, small particles of rock mix with rotted plant parts to provide minerals and other nutrients for the plants. The subsoil gives the roots of a plant something to hold onto. Bedrock holds the subsoil togcther.

Scoring Chart

Total Words Read in One Minute	Minus Words Missed	Total Words Read Correctly

KEY VOCABULARY

A Future Sculptor's Journal

Today we read about the rock **cycle.** I did not know that **solid** rocks start off as **liquid magma. Erosion, weathering,** and **pressure** can change one kind of rock into another. I think all rocks are related in some way. They belong to one big happy family!

Maybe when I grow up, I will be a sculptor. Then I can carve **layers** and layers of rocks all day long.

My first sculpture will be of Max.

Gem, Rock, and Mineral Stamps

Choose one country to research. Find out about the stamps that show rocks.

Countries with Gem, Rock, and Mineral Stamps

Afghanistan	Comoro Islands	New Caledonia
Algeria	Cyprus	New Zealand
Andorra	Ecuador	Norway
Angola	Fiji	Portugal
Armenia	Finland	Russia
Australia	France	Slovenia
Austria	French Polynesia	Spain
Azerbaijan	Germany	Sri Lanka
Belgium	Ghana	Switzerland
Botswana	Greenland	Tanzania
Brazil	Iceland	Thailand
Bulgaria	Israel	Tunisia
Burma	Kenya	Turkey
Canada	Kyrgyzstan	Uganda
Central African Republic	Macedonia	United States
Chile	Malawi	Uruguay
China	Monaco	Yugoslavia
Colombia	Namibia	Zimbabwe

Gems, Rocks, and Minerals on Stamps

agate	granite	pearl
amber	gypsum	quartz
amethyst	hematite	ruby
aquamarine	iron ore	sandstone
coal	jade	sapphire
copper	lapis lazuli	silver
diamond	malachite	sulfur
emerald	marble	topaz
garnet	mercury	tourmaline
gold	opal	zircon

Name ______________________ Date ____________

Experiment Record

Experiment Topic: ______________________

I wonder:
I guess the answer will be:
Materials for my experiment:
Steps I did in my experiment:
The results were:
My conclusion is:

Name ______________________ Date ____________

KWLQ Chart

K What I know	W What I want to learn	L What I learned	Q Questions I still have

Avenues
Writing Project Masters

Name ______________________ Date ______________

Features of a Biography

Read "In Gary Soto's Shoes."
Check the box if the biography has the feature.
Write the details.

Features	Does It Have the Feature?
The biography tells facts about the person's life.	☑ Yes. It says that Gary Soto published his first book in 1977.
The biography includes the dates of important events.	☐
It includes order words to tell when things happened.	☐
Each paragraph includes a main idea and supporting details.	☐
The order of the paragraphs makes sense.	☐

Name ______________________ Date ____________

Writing Project

Writing Prompt

Write a biography about an author. Give information about important events in the person's life.

1 Think of Ideas

Who are some authors you know about?
Which ones interest you?
Write the names.

Authors

1. Joseph Bruchac
2. ______________________
3. ______________________
4. ______________________
5. ______________________

2 Choose a Topic

Choose one person for your biography.
Circle the person's name.

Name ______________________________ Date ______________

Plan Your Biography

Write the name of the person.
Use the timeline to organize your research.

Name of Author: ______________________________

Dates	Events
________	______________________________
________	______________________________
________	______________________________
________	______________________________
________	______________________________
________	______________________________
________	______________________________
________	______________________________
________	______________________________

Name ______________________ Date ____________

Good Writing Trait: Organization

	Is the Whole Thing Organized?	Does the Writing Flow?
4 Wow! You have it!	❑ The writing is very well-organized. It fits the writer's purpose.	❑ The writing is very smooth. Each idea flows into the next one.
3 Good job!	❑ The writing is organized. It fits the writer's purpose.	❑ The writing is pretty smooth. There are only a few places where it jumps around.
2 Not quite	❑ The writing is organized, but it doesn't fit the writer's purpose.	❑ The writing jumps from one idea to another idea, but I can follow it a little.
1 Try again!	❑ The writing is not organized. Maybe the writer forgot to use a chart to plan.	❑ I can't tell what the writer wants to say.

Name ____________________ Date ____________

Write a Draft

Draw or paste a picture of the author in the box.
Start writing your draft below.
Keep writing on a separate sheet of paper.

Title: ____________________

Name the person.

Start with a main idea sentence.

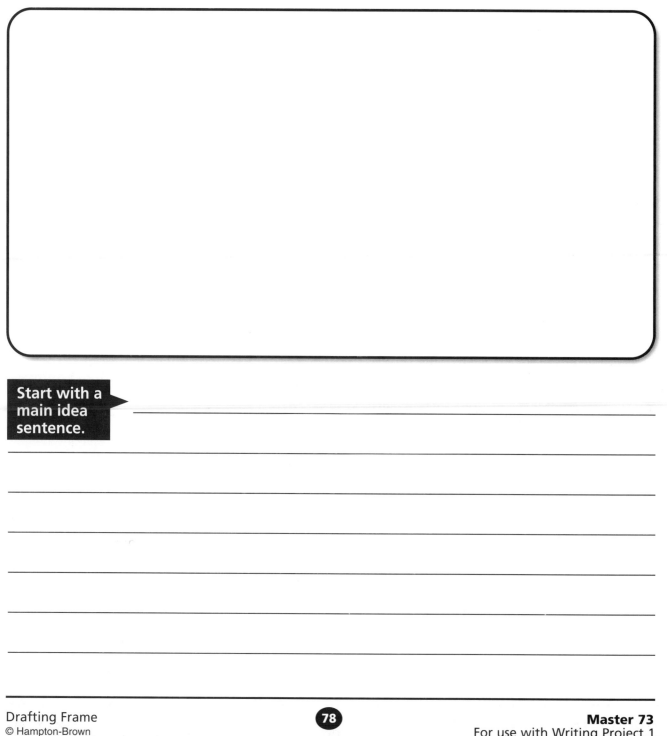

Name ______________________ Date ______________

Revise

Read the biography. Make changes to improve the organization and the sentences.

Revising Marks

Mark	Meaning
∧	Add.
	Take out.
	Change to this.
	Move to here.

Joseph Bruchac

Was born in 1942 in Saratoga Springs, New York. His grandparents raised him in Greenfield Center, New York. Bruchac helped. In his grandparents' store when he was young. His grandparents owned a general store in Greenfield Center.

In 1966, Bruchac and his wife moved to Ghana, West Africa. Bruchac taught English there for three years. Bruchac and his wife turned the old house and general store into an office. In 1969, the couple moved. Back to New York. Lived in the same house where Bruchac's grandparents had raised him. They started their own publishing company there.

Think About Organization

- ❑ Is the writing well-organized? Does it fit the writer's purpose?
- ❑ Does everything make sense?
- ❑ Is the writing smooth? Does one idea flow into the next one?

Name ______________________________ Date ______________

Edit and Proofread

Read the rest of the biography. Proofread for errors in capitalization, spelling, and punctuation. Use Proofreading Marks.

In 1997, joseph Bruchac wrote his autobiography, <u>bowman's store</u>. The book was named after his grandparents' Genral Store. In the book, Bruchac described his childhood in upstate New York when he was young, Bruchac did not know about his grandfather's Abenaki roots. he learned about his true backgrond as he got older. <u>Bowman's Store</u> won an Award. It was the Wordcraft Circle of Native Writers Prose Award.

Proofreading Marks

Mark	Meaning
∧	Add.
∧̣	Add a comma.
⊙	Add a period.
≡	Capitalize.
⬭	Check spelling.
/	Make lowercase.
⌒ℯ	Take out.

Name ______________________ Date ______________

Features of a Description

Read "The Big Storm."
Check the box if the writing has the feature.
Write the details.

Features	Does It Have the Feature?
The description has a title that tells what it is about.	☑ Yes. The title is "The Big Storm." All of the description tells about the storm.
The description tells what something ☐ looks like ☐ sounds like ☐ feels like	 ☐ ☐ ☐
Comparisons help the reader understand what is being described.	☐

Name ______________________ Date ____________

Writing Project

Writing Prompt

Write a description of a storm.
Include details to tell what the storm was like.

❶ Think of Ideas

What kinds of storms have you experienced?
What kinds of storms interest you? Make a list.

❷ Choose a Topic

Choose one kind of storm for your description. Circle it.

Name ____________________ Date ____________

Plan Your Description

Write the topic of your description in the center of the web. Then write interesting details around it.

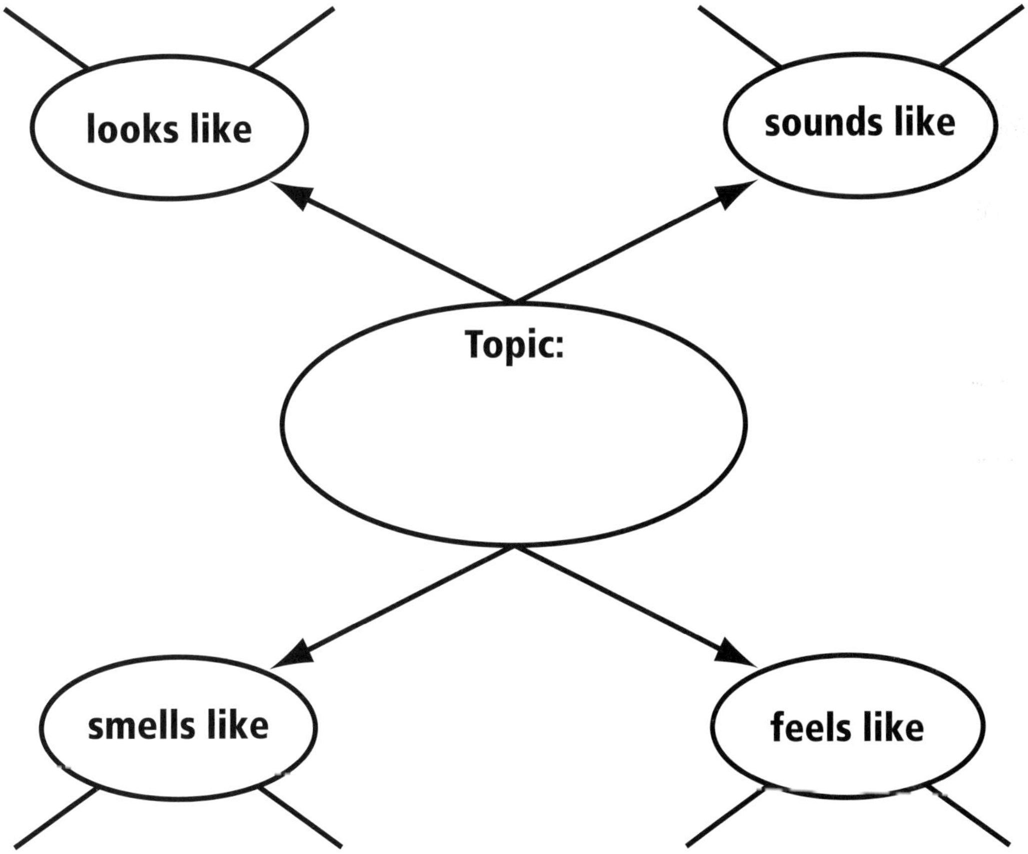

Name ______________________ Date ____________

Good Writing Trait: Development of Ideas

	Is the writing interesting and unusual?	How well do you understand the ideas?
4 **Wow! You have it!**	❑ The writer has thought about the topic carefully. ❑ The ideas are presented in a very interesting way.	❑ The writing answered all of my questions. There were enough details to help me understand.
3 **Good job!**	❑ The writer has thought about the topic. ❑ The ideas are presented in an interesting way.	❑ The writing answered most of my questions. There were enough details to help me understand.
2 **Not quite**	❑ The writer doesn't seem to have thought about the topic very much. ❑ The writing is OK, but not interesting.	❑ I have some questions that were not answered.
1 **Try again!**	❑ The writer doesn't seem to have thought about the topic at all. ❑ The ideas are presented in a boring way.	❑ I have a lot of questions. The writing didn't tell me enough.

Name ______________________________ Date ______________

Write a Draft

Start writing your description below. Keep writing on a separate sheet of paper if you need more room.

Title: ______________________________

Write a title that tells about the topic.

Start with a topic sentence.

Name ______________________ Date ____________

Revise

Read the description. Make changes to improve the ideas. Add colorful adjectives before the nouns and change plain verbs to more interesting action verbs.

Revising Marks

Mark	Meaning
∧	Add.
	Take out.
	Change to this.
	Move to here.

Thunderstorm!

A thunderstorm has lots of sights and sounds. First, clouds fill the sky. The clouds are a really dark color. The sky gets as dark as night.

Then a line goes through the sky—lightning! When you see lightning, you should go inside right away. It is not safe to be outside.

Now a boom follows the lightning. The heat of the lightning makes thunder. When thunder is close by, it can shake windows like an earthquake.

Think About Development of Ideas

- ❑ Has the writer thought about the topic carefully?
- ❑ Does the writing cover the topic fully?
- ❑ Are the ideas creative and interesting?
- ❑ Are there enough details to make the writing clear?

Edit and Proofread

Read the rest of the description. Check for errors in capitalization, spelling, and punctuation. Make sure that the subjects and verbs agree. Use Proofreading Marks.

Sometimes a thunderstorm makes heavy rains It is as if a trap door in the clouds opins up, The rain come pouring down. The heavy downpour sounds like a person druming. flash floods is possible if enough rain falls.

Strong winds can be part of a thunderstorm, too. They can blow at more than 50 miles per hour. Winds like these can do a lot of damage, such as knock down trees and power lines. They is very dangerus.

Proofreading Marks

Mark	Meaning
∧	Add.
⩘	Add a comma.
⊙	Add a period.
≡	Capitalize.
◯	Check spelling.
/	Make lowercase.
⸺ℯ	Take out.

Name ______________________ Date ____________

Features of a Personal Narrative

Read "A Good Luck Valentine."
Check the box if the narrative has the feature.
Write the details.

Features	Does It Have the Feature?
The personal narrative tells a true story. It tells about something that happened to the writer.	☑ Yes. The girl writes about her first Valentine's Day.
The personal narrative has a beginning, middle, and end.	☐
It uses the words *I*, *me*, and *my*.	☐
It includes describing words to tell how the writer felt.	☐
The writing sounds real. You can tell something about who the writer is.	☐

Name ______________________ Date ____________

Writing Project

Writing Prompt

Write a personal narrative about something special your family has. Share an experience you have had with this special thing.

1 Think of Ideas

What special things does your family have?
Why are they special to you? Write your ideas.

2 Choose a Topic

Choose one idea for the topic of your personal narrative. Circle it.

Name ______________________ Date ______________

Plan Your Narrative

Write the title of your personal narrative.
Then plan the parts. Use a story map.

Title: ______________________

Beginning

↓

Middle

↓

End

Name ______________________ Date ____________

Good Writing Trait: Voice

	Does the writing sound real?	Do the words fit the purpose and audience?
4 **Wow! You have it!**	❑ The writing shows who the writer is. ❑ The writer seems to be talking right to me.	❑ The writer uses words that really fit the purpose and audience.
3 **Good job!**	❑ The writing shows who the writer is. ❑ The writer does a good job sounding real.	❑ The writer uses good words for the purpose and audience.
2 **Not quite**	❑ It's hard to tell who the writer is. ❑ The writer doesn't seem to be talking to me.	❑ The writer uses some words that fit the purpose and audience.
1 **Try again!**	❑ I can't tell who the writer is. ❑ The writer doesn't seem to care.	❑ The words don't fit the purpose or audience.

Name ____________________ Date ____________

Write a Draft

Start writing your personal narrative below. Use a separate sheet of paper if you need more room.

Title: ____________________

Name ______________________________ Date ______________

Revise

Read the personal narrative. Make changes to improve the voice of the writing. Replace the underlined words with more interesting words.

Revising Marks

Mark	Meaning
	Add.
	Take out.
	Change to this.
	Move to here.

Our Kachina Doll

One day my mom gave me a doll. It looked very different. I had never seen a thing like it. My mom said it was a Kachina doll. That doll was part of our Hopi background, she said. She told me the doll had belonged to my grandmother.

I wanted to learn more about the Kachina doll. My mom said I would have to wait until the following weekend. Then we'd take a trip with the doll. I felt really good! I could hardly wait for the weekend to come.

Think About Voice

- ❑ Is the writer speaking to you?
- ❑ Does the writer seem to care about the ideas?
- ❑ Are words and phrases interesting?
- ❑ Do the words fit the purpose and audience?

Name ______________________________ Date ________________

Edit and Proofread

Read the rest of the personal narrative. Check for errors in capitalization, spelling, and punctuation. Make sure that pronouns are used correctly. Use Proofreading Marks.

The next weekend, my hole family went to a Kachina ceremony. Me took the Kachina doll along. One man was dressed in a costume like our Kachina doll. She told us that our Kachina was an Eagle Kachina. then the man showed us the dance of the Eagle Kachina They was Beautiful, the way he swooped and cried out likc an eagle. I'm so prowd of my Kachina doll now.

Proofreading Marks

Mark	Meaning
∧	Add.
∧ (with comma)	Add a comma.
⊙	Add a period.
≡	Capitalize.
⬭	Check spelling.
/	Make lowercase.
⌇ (delete mark)	Take out.

Name ______________________ Date ______________

Features of Realistic Fiction

Read "Rows and Piles of Coins."
Check the box if the story has the feature.
Write the details.

Features	Does It Have the Feature?
The story has a plot with events that could really happen.	☑ Yes. A boy could really save coins to buy a bicycle.
The story has a realistic setting. The time and place could be real.	☐
The characters could be real people.	☐
The story feels complete. It has a: ☐ beginning ☐ middle ☐ end	 ☐ ☐ ☐

Name ______________________ Date ____________

Writing Project

Writing Prompt

Write a realistic fiction story about a character who saves money to buy something special.

1 Think of Ideas

What special things might someone save money to buy? Write your ideas.

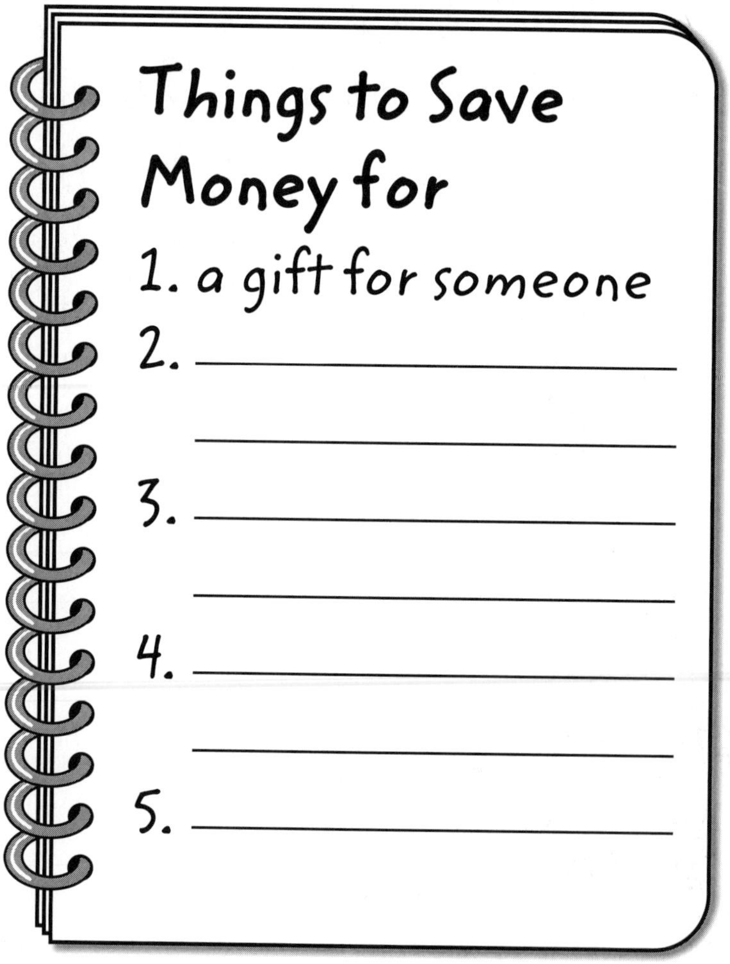

2 Choose a Topic

Choose one idea for your story. Circle it.

Name ______________________________ Date ______________

Plan Your Story

Make a story map. Plan the goal, events, and outcome.

Title: ______________________________

Goal:

Event 1:

Event 2:

Event 3:

Outcome:

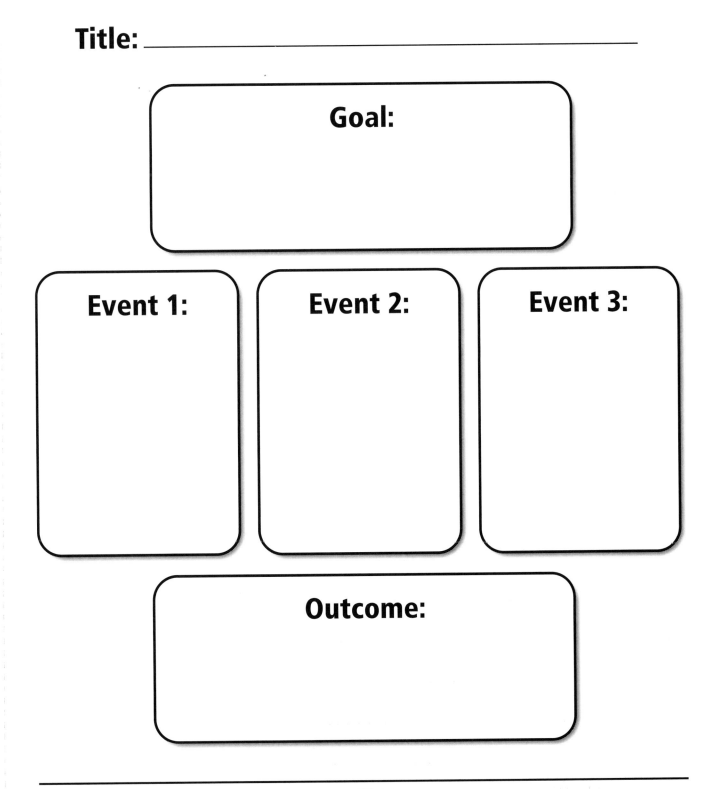

Name ______________________ Date ______________

Good Writing Trait: Focus and Coherence

	Are the Ideas Related?	Is the Writing Complete?
4 **Wow! You have it!**	❑ All of the ideas are about one topic.	❑ There is a beginning and an end. ❑ All of the details in the middle are important.
3 **Good job!**	❑ Most of the ideas are about one topic.	❑ There is a beginning and an end. ❑ Most of the details in the middle are important.
2 **Not quite**	❑ There are many ideas that don't go together. It is hard to tell what the writing is all about.	❑ The writing has a beginning or an end, but it doesn't have both. ❑ Some of the details in the middle don't belong there.
1 **Try again!**	❑ The ideas don't go together. I can't tell what the writing is really about.	❑ The writing does not have a beginning. ❑ The writing does not have an end.

Name ______________________ Date ______________

Write a Draft

Start writing your story below. Keep writing on a separate sheet of paper.

Title: ______________________

Name ______________________________ Date ______________

Revise

Read the story. Make changes to improve it. Take out ideas and details that don't belong. Combine two sentences in each paragraph.

Revising Marks

Mark	Meaning
∧	Add.
	Take out.
	Change to this.
	Move to here.

A Gift for Grandmother

Loc is looking for a present for his grandmother. He knows that his grandmother likes flowers. His grandfather is a teacher. Loc goes to the gift shop. He sees a glass vase. Loc thinks the vase is the perfect gift for his grandmother. The vase costs twenty-five dollars.

Loc goes home. He gets his piggy bank. He counts the money he has saved. Loc only has a few dollars saved. Loc has a younger sister. He tries to think of a plan to get more money.

The first thing Loc does is easy. He puts the money back in his Piggy Bank. He decides not to spend any on comic books.

Think About Focus and Coherence

- ❏ Are all of the ideas about one topic?
- ❏ Is there a beginning and an end?
- ❏ Are all of the details in the middle important?

Name ______________________ Date ______________

Edit and Proofread

Read the rest of the story. Check for errors in capitalization, spelling, and punctuation. Use Proofreading Marks.

Loc gets another idea. He can earn money! He nocks on his neighbor's Door. "Do you need someone to shovel the snow in your driveway, he asks mr. Porter.

Loc's neighbor pays him five dollars to shovel the snow. When he is done at Mr. porter's house, Loc is not tired He is excited so he knocks on more doors. Loc shovels snow for two more neighbors.

Wow Now Loc has earned fiveteen dollars. He worked hard and now he can buy the gift for his grandmother.

Proofreading Marks

Mark	Meaning
∧	Add.
∧ with a comma	Add a comma.
⊙	Add a period.
≡	Capitalize.
⬭	Check spelling.
/	Make lowercase.
delete loop	Take out.

Avenues

Student Writing Samples

STUDENT WRITING SAMPLE

Read this story.
Think about how well it is written.
Give it a score. Circle the number.

Focus and Coherence

Score

1 2 3 4

The Field Trip

One day at school, Hector's teacher held up a small plastic dinosaur. It was a brown Brontosaurus. The teacher said the dinosaur was a clue about their next field trip. She wanted the students to guess where they might be going.

Everyone named a different place. No one guessed the right place until Tina said, "Are we going to the Science Museum? I know there's a new dinosaur exhibit there."

That was the right guess. The next week, the class got on the bus and rode to the Science Museum. They had studied dinosaurs in books, but here was their chance to see life-size models!

At the museum, the class had a guide who knew all about dinosaurs. He let the students wander around the exhibit and look at the models. Then he gave a talk about each one.

When the guide was finished talking, the students had a chance to ask questions. Hector wanted to know how fast Tyrannosaurus rex could run. Tina wanted to know how big Stegosaurus' eggs were. Everyone had a question, and the guide answered them all. Then it was time to go back to school.

The next day, the students thanked their teacher for the field trip. They told her they had learned a lot in one day. Hector wanted to know where they would go for their next field trip. The teacher just smiled and held up a starfish.

STUDENT WRITING SAMPLE

Read this story.
Think about how well it is written.
Give it a score. Circle the number.

Focus and Coherence			
Score			
1	2	3	4

Pet Day

Sakura put her cat, Grumpy, in the cat carrier. It was Pet Day at school. Sakura was so happy about bringing Grumpy to school. She knew that he would have a good time.

Sakura thought that Grumpy was a better pet than a dog. Dogs were noisy and liked to run around chasing squirrels. Grumpy was a nice, quiet pet. He liked to eat tuna fish.

Sakura's mom drove Sakura and Grumpy to school. Sakura's friends brought their pets, too. Manuel had a fish in a small tank. Josh had a hamster. Lena had a dog on a leash. The dog was barking!

At the end of the day, Sakura's mom was going to pick up Sakura and Grumpy. Mr. Lee, her teacher, wrote the students' names on the board. He said they would share their pets in that order. Sakura's name was near the end.

The students shared their pets. When it was Sakura's turn, she opened the cat carrier. Grumpy jumped right out and ran toward Lena's barking dog! The dog got away from Lena and chased Grumpy around the room!

Now all the students and Mr. Lee chased Grumpy and Lena's dog. At last, Mr. Lee caught Grumpy. He handed the cat to Sakura. Lena got her dog back. Then the bell rang. Everyone was glad that school was over and the pets could go home.

STUDENT WRITING SAMPLE

Read this story.
Think about how well it is written.
Give it a score. Circle the number.

Focus and Coherence

Score			
1	2	3	4

The Science Fair

Every year, Todd's school has a Science Fair. This year there will be a Science Fair, too. Todd has to think of a science project. Each fifth-grader must have a project in the Science Fair.

Todd likes science, but his favorite subject is reading. He likes to read biographies of sports heroes. He also likes to read books of riddles. Then he asks his friends the riddles. He can usually fool his friends with them.

Todd thinks he might do his science project on the rain forest. He could make a diorama with little clay models of the animals who live there. He could tell people ways to save the rain forests. Todd will ask his teacher if that is a good idea.

Todd's teacher is Ms. Hill. She teaches science three days a week. Right now, the class is learning about the planets and stars. They might take a field trip to an observatory.

The Science Fair is three weeks away. Ms. Hill likes Todd's idea about the rain forest. She tells him to get started. He goes to the library. He uses encyclopedias and the Internet. In three weeks, Todd's rain forest project is finished.

The Science Fair is in the gym. The basketball team plays games in the gym. Todd's rain forest project is set up on a table. Ms. Hill and the other teachers look at it. They tell Todd he did a good job.

STUDENT WRITING SAMPLE

Read this story.
Think about how well it is written.
Give it a score. Circle the number.

Focus and Coherence

Score

1 2 3 4

The Car Wash

Ishana's school had a car wash to raise money for new computers. The fourth-grade students washed cars on Saturday. That was last Saturday. Ishana is in the fourth grade.

Some of the parents and teachers helped. They got hoses and buckets. They got sponges and soap. A lot of adults are usually busy on Saturdays. They helped wash and dry cars all day. The car wash cost five dollars for each car.

The school needed new computers. There was only one computer in the library and it was very old. Also, it was too hard to share one computer. The teachers wanted to have a new computer in each classroom. The parents said, "Let's have a car wash. We can raise money for the new computers."

Some parents wanted to collect cans and bottles. They said it was a good way to get money. And it helped save the earth because it was recycling, too. Some parents didn't like that idea. They said there was no room at the school to keep all those cans and bottles.

Last year, the school had a bake sale. The bake sale was in the cafeteria. The bake sale raised money for library books. Some of the parents and students baked cakes, cookies, and pies. Ishana baked brownies. Most people bought chocolate chip cookies. The bake sale raised a lot of money, so the library got a lot of new books.

STUDENT WRITING SAMPLE

Read this report.
Think about how well it is written.
Give it a score. Circle the number

Organization			
Score			
1	2	3	4

Volcanoes

A volcano starts as an opening in the Earth's crust. The opening is called a vent. Hot, melted rock forms deep below the Earth's surface. The melted rock is called magma. It pushes through the vent in the Earth's crust. When the magma reaches the air, it is called lava. The lava pours out and starts to cool off. It forms a cone, or mountain. Each time the volcano erupts, the lava builds up and the volcano gets bigger.

Some of the world's volcanoes are above sea level, but most are below the sea. Some islands, such as the Hawaiian Islands, arc actually the tops of undersea volcanoes.

Volcanoes can be active, dormant, or extinct. An active volcano erupts often. A dormant volcano does not erupt a lot. An extinct volcano has stopped erupting.

Active volcanoes can be dangerous to people. Lava flows and ash can damage or destroy property. Sometimes volcanoes cause earthquakes or giant sea waves called tsunamis. These natural disasters can injure or kill people.

Today scientists try to predict when a volcano will erupt. They measure small earthquakes caused by moving magma. They measure gas that is released when the magma gets near the Earth's surface. Scientists watch volcanoes closely so they can warn people to get away.

STUDENT WRITING SAMPLE

Read this report.
Think about how well it is written.
Give it a score. Circle the number.

Organization			
Score			
1	2	3	4

Earthquakes

The Earth's crust is made up of huge sections called plates. The plates are made of rock. The plates are always moving. They move very slowly. Sometimes the plates move sideways and sometimes they move up and down.

The crack between two plates is called a fault. Most earthquakes happen along faults, when two plates run into each other. This makes waves of energy. The waves travel through the ground, making it shake. I was in an earthquake once. It was scary!

The San Andreas fault is in California. This fault is more than 800 miles long. In some places, it is more than ten miles deep.

Every day there are thousands of earthquakes around the world. Most are so small that no one notices them. Scientists measure earthquakes with special equipment. They give each earthquake a number on the Richter scale. Charles Richter developed the Richter scale in 1935. Richter worked at the California Institute of Technology. The number tells the strength of the earthquake. People can't feel an earthquake that measures 0 on the scale, but they can feel one that is 4 or higher.

Earthquakes, hurricanes, and other disasters happen all over the world. Earthquakes can do a lot of damage. They can knock down buildings, and cause landslides. They are one of nature's most powerful forces.

STUDENT WRITING SAMPLE

Read this story.
Think about how well it is written.
Give it a score. Circle the number.

Development of Ideas			
Score			
1	2	3	4

The Day the Sky Turned Green

"Boy, it sure is warm. It's like summer!" my mom said one day in March. Suddenly the sky seemed too dark. My mother told us to come inside right away. There was a tornado warning. I looked over the flat land around us. All I saw was that the dark sky had turned a strange color. "Green?" I said to myself. "I didn't know the sky could be green."

When we were all inside, Mom made us go to the basement. She brought bottled water, snacks, flashlights, and a radio. We crawled under the dusty stairs and waited. The world seemed silent. I could hear my little sister breathing next to me. I put my arm around her so she wouldn't be scared.

Then we heard a loud roar. It sounded like a train was coming! Suddenly we could feel the house shaking above us. The roaring got louder and louder. I thought it would never stop. Then we heard banging and crashing, as though the whole house was coming apart. My sister screamed. I did, too. The terrible sounds scared us all.

Within minutes, the roar died down. The tornado was going away. We could a hear a few small things rolling around upstairs.

When Mom said it was safe, we crept upstairs and opened the door. We stood there, looking up at the bright blue sky. We hugged and laughed and cried. Our roof was gone, but we were all okay!

STUDENT WRITING SAMPLE

Read this personal narrative.
Think about how well it is written.
Give it a score. Circle the number.

Voice			
Score			
1	2	3	4

The Soccer Team

On Monday, I saw a big sign at school. The sign said: "Try out for the soccer team Friday at 3:00." The minute I saw that sign, I knew I had to do it. Soccer is my favorite sport! I play soccer all the time with my cousins. I never miss a game on TV. I dream of being a professional soccer player someday.

I asked my cousin Rafael to help me get ready for the tryout. Every day after school, we ran up and down the soccer field. We kicked the ball back and forth and practiced our headers. I thought I might get a dent in my head from passing so many balls!

On Friday at 3:00, I went to the soccer field. The coach was Mr. Posada. He was also our gym teacher. I liked him because he always told jokes and made us laugh.

Mr. Posada made us run drills. Then he put us on teams and asked us to play a game. He took a lot of notes in his notebook. After three hours, the tryout was over. Mr. Posada said he would post the names of the team members on Monday.

On Monday, I saw the sheet of paper on the wall. My heart pounded. I held my breath and went over to read the names. Would mine be there? I couldn't think. I just had to look. Halfway down the list, I saw my name. I was on the team! Wait until Rafael and my family heard the good news. I could hardly believe it myself.

STUDENT WRITING SAMPLE

Read this story.
Think about how well it is written.
Give it a score. Circle the number.

Development of Ideas			
Score			
1	2	3	4

The Flood

There was a big flood in my town. I saw my grandmother outside. A firefighter carried Grandmama through the water. I watched from the upstairs window.

The sirens were loud. I covered my ears. Then I stopped because I wanted to hear what the firefighter was shouting. The firefighter told us to wait in the house. He said they could come back in a boat.

My family and I waited. We saw Grandmama going away in a truck with a lot of other people.

Pretty soon, the firefighters came back to the house. My sister and I got into one boat. Our mother got into the other boat.

Later, I looked around at the people in the shelter. Everyone was wet, tired, and worried. It seemed like the whole town was there.

Finally, my family got to go back to our house. Everything was damaged. People had to clean the mud and stains off everything in their houses. Later, everything went back to normal, but I will never forget the flood.

STUDENT WRITING SAMPLE

Read this story.
Think about how well it is written.
Give it a score. Circle the number.

Development of Ideas			
Score			
1	2	3	4

Blizzard Conditions

My big brother Rico ran out to the car. The rest of us were waiting inside it. Rico had his new driver's license, and he was going to take all the kids for a ride.

"It's supposed to snow again today," he said.

Where we grew up, the weather was hot all the time. We swam a lot and went to the beach. Here in our new home, there is snow and ice all winter long.

Rico backed the car out of the driveway and headed into the country. The snow was piled high. There was a cold wind, but we didn't care.

Suddenly, the wind got stronger. Snow started blowing across the road and across our windshield.

Rico stopped the car. He couldn't see anymore! He put on emergency flashers. We were scared. All around us was snow. The car was dark inside. It was very scary! We waited in the car and hoped the storm would stop.

Finally, it slowed down, and we could see out again. A woman with a snow plow came by. She said, "So is this your first blizzard?"

"Yes," we all yelled. She laughed and said to check the whole weather report next time.

STUDENT WRITING SAMPLE

Read this story.
Think about how well it is written.
Give it a score. Circle the number.

Focus and Coherence			
Score			
1	2	3	4

After the Hurricane

Drip, drip, drip. I could hear the raindrops as they fell from the roof. At least the roof is still there, I thought.

Seconds later, my dad opened the door to the closet. It was not a very big place. My whole family had been hiding there, ever since we heard that a hurricane was coming.

My mother, father, brother, and I climbed up from the floor of the closet. We were sore from sitting for so long and from being so scared and tense. Slowly, we all looked around. Our dog got out of the closet, too.

The house didn't look the same at all! There was nothing on the walls. The furniture was turned over and torn or broken. Everywhere, there was trash. Torn-up paper, and broken pieces of our stuff were lying all around. The doors and all the windows were gone. Broken glass was everywhere. Air blew through the house.

The entire floor was covered in about three inches of water. My brother and I held hands with our parents. The walls and the furniture and trash lying around were all wet, too. It was like we had a rainstorm inside the house!

When we went in the kitchen, we saw that all the cupboards were open. They were empty, too. What will we eat? I thought.

I was right to worry! We didn't find anything to eat for a day and a half!

STUDENT WRITING SAMPLE

Read this personal narrative.
Think about how well it is written.
Give it a score. Circle the number.

Voice

Score

1 2 3 4

Learning English

English is a hard language to learn. I know because I am trying to learn English right now. There are so many new sounds and words to learn, and some words mean more than one thing! That's hard.

My teacher's name is Ms. Madduri. She has patience. On the first day of class, she gave each of us a dictionary. It had words in both Spanish and English. She said, "When you get stuck, check in the dictionary." I use my dictionary all the time.

We talk about many different things in class. Sometimes we talk about the weather or our families or our favorite books. Each week one of the students has to give a show-and-tell talk. Once a month we take a trip somewhere.

Ms. Madduri asks us questions to help us practice speaking. She says we should try to speak English every chance we get. "Practice makes perfect" is Ms. Madduri's motto. I believe it's a very good motto.

I practice speaking English with my friends Brian and Cathy. They are a big help because they help me with some of the tricky words. There are a lot of tricky words.

I will work hard at learning English. One day I will be able to speak English in a good way, thanks to Ms. Madduri and my friends.

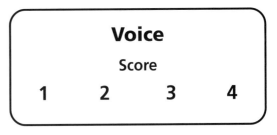

STUDENT WRITING SAMPLE

Read this personal narrative.
Think about how well it is written.
Give it a score. Circle the number.

Voice

Score

1 2 3 4

Big News

One day my mother came home from work. She was excited. She told me she had some news. She had a new job. It was in another state. "We will move to a new house, and you will go to a new school," she said.

I was sad and excited at the same time. There were lots of things I was going to miss at my old school, like my friends and playing on the softball team. I would miss my math teacher, Ms. Hart.

Then my mother told me about my new school. She said it had a pool. I could ride my bike to school. I could join the math club. My mother said I would like the new school.

My mother said we would move at the end of the school year. That way I could finish fourth grade in my old school. It would be easier to start at a new school in September.

Everyone knew I was moving at the end of the year. They were nice to me. They said they would write to me. They might even come to visit me in the summer, too.

On the last day of school, my teacher and friends had a good-bye party for me. They had balloons and a cake. They gave me a book of photos and wrote "good luck." That was nice.

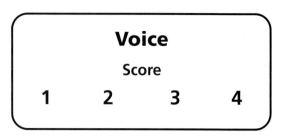

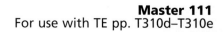

STUDENT WRITING SAMPLE

Read this personal narrative.
Think about how well it is written.
Give it a score. Circle the number.

Voice

Score

1 2 3 4

The School Band

I play the clarinet. I have played the clarinet since I was seven years old. First, Ms. Price was my teacher. Now I have lessons with Mr. Johnson. I practice all the time. On the weekends I spend a lot of time practicing.

This year I am in fifth grade. In fifth grade, students can try out for the school band. Band members wear a blue uniform. They have to practice a lot and stay after school.

The band tryouts are next week. I have to play a song for Ms. Summers. She is the band director. If I play well and don't make any mistakes, then maybe Ms. Summers will ask me to join the band. I don't know yet what song I'm going to play.

Last year, my brother tried out for the band. He plays the trumpet. Ms. Summers liked my brother's playing. So now my brother is in the band.

The band gets to play in the holiday concerts at our school. The band also marches in the Memorial Day parade. That is in May. It would be nice to be in the band.

Avenues

Family Newsletters

Avenues NEWSLETTER

UNIT 1

Online with Gary Soto

Stay in Touch!

In this unit, we explore communications.

1. How do you stay in touch with friends and family who live far away? Make a list of all the ways.

____

____

____

2. Have you ever used e-mail? Talk about how this might change families and even cultures of people who live in different countries.

What We're Reading

"If the Shoe Fits"

In this story, a boy learns the value of sharing.

"In Gary Soto's Shoes"

A biography tells about author Gary Soto, and the author answers e-mail from his readers.

____

____

____

____

____

____

____

____

____

BOLETÍN Avenues

¡Escríbeme!

En esta unidad, hablaremos de las comunicaciones.

1. ¿Cómo se comunican ustedes con amigos y familiares que viven lejos? Hagan una lista de todas las maneras.
2. ¿Alguna vez han usado el correo electrónico? ¿Cómo podría este sistema de comunicación afectar a las familias que viven en distintos países?

Estamos leyendo...

"A la medida"

En este cuento, un niño aprende el valor de compartir.

"Los zapatos de Gary Soto"

Una biografía habla del autor Gary Soto, y él contesta correo electrónico de sus lectores.

TIN THƯ Avenues

TÍN CHỈ 1 | **Lên Mạng Với Gary Soto**

Giữ Liên Lạc Với Nhau!

Trong tín chỉ này, chúng ta khám phá về sự thông tin liên lạc.

1. Quý vị giữ liên lạc với bạn bè và gia đình sống xa nơi quý vị ở như thế nào? Liệt kê ra tất cả những phương thức.

___

___

___

2. Có bao giờ quý vị sử dụng thư điện tử (e-mail) không? Nói về cách phương tiện truyền thông này có thể thay đổi các gia đình và ngay cả các nền văn hóa của con người sống tại nhiều quốc gia trên thế giới như thế nào.

___

___

___

___

___

___

___

___

___

Chúng Ta Đang Đọc Những Gì

"Nếu Giày Vừa Chân"

Trong chuyện này, một cậu bé học được giá trị của sự chia xẻ.

"Trong Vị Thế Của Gary Soto"

Bài tiểu sử kể về tác giả Gary Soto, và tác giả trả lời thư điện tử (e-mail) cho độc giả của mình.

Avenues 教育通讯

保持联系!

在这一单元里，我们将探讨通讯知识。

1. 你怎样与远方的家人和朋友保持联系的？写出所有联系的方式。

2. 你是否使用过电子邮件？讨论一下电子邮件能够给家庭，甚至给生活在不同国度、不同文化的人们带来的变化。

读书目录

《鞋子合适吗?》
在这个故事里，一个男孩理解了共同分享的价值。

《假如你是盖瑞 · 索岛》
这一传记讲述了作者盖瑞 · 索岛 (Gary Soto) 和他回答读者的电子邮件。

Avenues 뉴스레터

연락 잊지 마세요!

이 유닛에서는 의사소통에 대하여 배웁니다.

1. 멀리 있는 친구나 가족들과 어떻게 소식을 주고 받나요? 그 방법들을 모두 열거해 보세요.

____

____

____

2. 이메일을 사용해 본적이 있나요? 이메일이 가족들은 물론 심지어는 다른 나라에 사는 사람들과의 문화에 어떤 영향을 끼치는가 말해보세요.

우리가 읽고 있는 책들

"신발이 맞으면"
한 소년이 나눔의 가치를 배운다.

"개리 소토의 신발"
작가 개리 소토의 소개와 작가가 독자들의 문의를 이메일로 답한다.

____

____

____

____

____

____

____

____

____

Nco Ntsoov Nug Moo!

Nyob rau tshoojntawv no, peb yuav tshawb kawm txog kev sib tham sib xa xov.

1. Ua li cas koj thiaj paub txog tej phoojywg thiab koj tsevneeg uas nyob deb deb ntawm koj moo? Sau tej kev sib tham sib nug moo uas koj siv ntawd rau hauv qab no.

2. Koj puas tau siv dua e-mail? Tham txog tias e-mail yuav ua rau tsevneeg tej neej hloov li cas, tsis tag li, tseem yuav ua rau cov neeg nyob txawv teb txawv chaw tej kev coj noj coj ua hloov.

Tej Peb Nyeem Txog

"Yog Txhais Khau Haum"

Hauv zaj lus no, tus menyuam tub kawm txog tus txiajncim ntawm kam txawj sib faib siv sib faib ua.

"Nyob Rau Gary Soto Txhais Khau"

Cov lus piav txog tus kws sau ntawv Gary Soto lub neej, thiab txog tej nws teb cov neeg nyeem nws cov ntawv tej e-mail uas lawv xa rau nws.

BILTEN Avenues

Ann Kenbe Kontak la!

Nan leson sa a, nou pral chèche konprann kominikasyon.

1. Kijan ou kenbe kontak ak zanmi epi fanmi ou ki viv lwen ou? Fè yon lis sou tout jan ou kenbe kontak avèk yo.

2. Èske ou janm sèvi ak imèl? Pale kijan sa ka chanje fanmi ak tout kilti moun ki viv nan diferan peyi.

Kisa Nap Li

"Si Se Pou Ou"

Nan ti istwa sa a yon ti gason ap aprann konnen vale pataje ak lòt

"Nan Plas Gary Soto"

Men yon istwa sou lavi ekriven Gary Soto; epi li reponn moun ki li liv li yo pa imèl.

Why Is the Sky So High?

In this unit, we will read a folk tale that tells why people see stars in the sky.

1. With your child, share a folk tale that tells why or how something came to be. How did you learn the story?
2. Have your child draw a picture on the back of this page to remind him or her about the story.
3. Help your child take notes about the story. Remind your child to bring the notes and picture to class.

What We're Reading

"Pushing Up the Sky"

This play, based on a Native American folk tale, tells why people see stars in the sky.

"Native Homes"

This social studies article explores homes of Native people in America.

¿Por qué está tan lejos el cielo?

En esta unidad, leeremos un cuento tradicional que explica por qué se ven estrellas en el cielo.

1. Comparta con su hijo o hija un cuento tradicional que explique el porqué de una cosa. ¿Cómo aprendió usted el cuento?
2. Pida a su hijo o hija que, al otro lado de esta hoja, haga un dibujo que le recuerde el cuento.
3. Ayude a su hijo o hija a tomar notas. Recuérdele que debe traer esta hoja a la clase.

Estamos leyendo...

"Empujando el cielo"

Esta obra de teatro, basada en un cuento tradicional de la cultura indígena americana, explica por qué hay estrellas en el cielo.

"Viviendas indígenas"

Este artículo de ciencias sociales explora las viviendas de los indígenas americanos.

TIN THƯ Avenues

TÍN CHỈ 2 | **Quê Hương Đất Nước**

Tại Sao Bầu Trời Quá Cao?

Trong tín chỉ này, chúng ta sẽ đọc một chuyện cổ tích kể tại sao người ta nhìn thấy những vì sao trên nền trời.

1. Kể cho con của quý vị nghe một chuyện cổ tích nói tại sao hay bằng cách nào một vật nào đó có mặt trên đời. Làm sao quý vị biết được chuyện này.
2. Bảo con của quý vị vẽ một bức tranh trên mặt sau của tờ giấy này để nhắc em nhớ về câu chuyện này.
3. Giúp con của quý vị ghi chú lại câu chuyện. Nhắc em mang lời ghi chú và bức tranh vào lớp học.

Chúng Ta Đang Đọc Những Gì

"Đẩy Lên Bầu Trời"

Vở kịch này dựa vào một chuyện cổ tích của người Mỹ Bản Xứ kể vì sao con người nhìn thấy các vì sao trên trời.

"Nhà Của Người Bản Xứ"

Bài báo nghiên cứu về xã hội này khám phá về nhà ở của người dân bản xứ tại châu Mỹ.

Avenues 教育通讯

为什么天空这样高？

我们将在这一单元里，阅读一篇有关人们为什么看到星星的传说。

1. 与你的孩子分享一个民间故事，这个故事应包含着某事物的前因和后果。你是怎么知道这个故事的？
2. 让你的孩子在这张纸的背面画下这个故事的大意。
3. 帮助你的孩子记下这个故事要点并提醒孩子上课时带笔记和画的图画。

读书目录

《撑起天空》

这个根据美国土著人传说改编的戏剧讲述了人们如何理解天空里的星星。

《土著人的家》

这一篇社会调查文章探讨了美国土著人的家。

Avenues 뉴스레터

하늘은 왜 그렇게 높은가?

이 유닛에서는 아메리칸 인디언 전설을 통하여 사람들이 왜 하늘의 별들을 쳐다보았는지를 배웁니다.

1. 인디언 전설을 통하여 어떻게 그리고 왜 별들이 만들어졌는가 배우십시오. 이야기를 즐기셨나요?
2. 이야기와 관련하여 페이지 뒷면에 그림을 그리라고 하십시오.
3. 이야기의 내용을 적으라고 하십시오. 그림과 적은 것을 클래스에 갖고 가라고 하십시오.

우리가 읽고있는 책들

"하늘 밀어올리기"

아메리칸 인디언들의 전설로서, 왜 사람들이 하늘의 별들을 보는지 얘기한다.

"원주민의 집"

아메리칸 인디언들의 주거 형식들을 설명한다.

Vim Li Cas Lub Ntuj Thiaj Li Nyob Siab Heev?

Nyob rau tshoojntawv no, peb yuav nyeem txog zaj dabneeg uas qhia txog tias vim li cas neeg thiaj li pom hnub qub nyob saum ntuj.

1. Qhia rau koj tus menyuam txog ib zaj dabneeg uas hais txog tias yog vim li cas thiaj muaj yam khoom ntawd los yog qhov chaw ntawd. Ua cas koj thiaj paub txog zaj dabneeg ntawd?
2. Hais kom koj tus menyuam kos ib daim duab rau daim nplooj ntawv no sab nrauv kom pab nws nco tau zaj dab neeg no.
3. Pab koj tus menyuam muab zaj dabneeg sau rau hauv ntawv. Nco ntsoov hais kom koj tus menyuam nqa daim ntawd sau tau thiab daim duab tuaj tom nws chav tsev kawmntawv.

Tej Peb Nyeem Txog

"Thawb Lub Ntuj Kom Siab"

Zaj yeebyam no piav txog cov Khab Asmeslivkas zaj dabneeg uas qhia txog tias vim cas neeg thiaj li pom hnub qub nyob saum ntuj.

"Tej Qub Teb Qub Chaw Yug Yus"

Tsab ntawv qhia txog kev haumxeeb (social studies) yuav pab peb tshawb kawm txog cov neeg ib txhiab ib txhis nyob rau thooj av Asmeslivkas (Native people in America).

BILTEN Avenues

Poukisa Syèl la Wo Konsa?

Nan leson sa a, nou pral li yon ti kont ki eksplike poukisa moun wè zetwal nan syèl la.

1. Pataje yon kont ak pitit ou a ki di poukisa oubyen kijan sèten bagay te fèt. Kijan ou te aprann istwa sa a?
2. Fè pitit ou a desinen yon imaj sou do fèy sa a pou li ka sonje ti istwa sa a.
3. Ede pitit ou pran nòt sou istwa sa a. Fè pitit ou a sonje pou li pote nòt yo ak imaj la nan klas la.

Kisa Nap Li

"Monte Syèl La Piwo"

Pyès teyat sa a baze sou yon kont Natif Natal Ameriken ki eksplike poukisa moun wè zetwal nan syèl la.

"Kay Moun Natif Natal Yo"

Atik syans sosyal sa a pale de kay Moun Natif Natal nan peyi Lamerik.

Weather Song

In this unit, we will learn about weather.

1. Share a poem, song, or saying about weather that you learned as a child.
2. Have your child draw a picture on the back of this page to remind him or her about the meaning of the poem or song.
3. Help your child write down the poem or song. Remind your child to bring the notes and picture to class.

What We're Reading

"Twister"

In this story, a family survives a tornado.

"The Big Storm"

This news article tells about a huge storm that swept across the U.S. in 1982.

Canción del clima

En esta unidad, aprenderemos sobre el clima.

1. Comparta un poema, canción o dicho sobre el clima que usted aprendió en su niñez.
2. Pida a su hijo o hija que, al otro lado de esta hoja, dibuje algo que le ayude a recordar el poema o la canción.
3. Ayude a su hijo o hija a escribir la letra del poema o la canción. Recuérdele que debe traer esta hoja a la clase.

Estamos leyendo...

"Tornado"

En este cuento, una familia sobrevive un tornado.

"La gran tormenta"

Este artículo noticiero describe una gran tormenta que arrasó con los Estados Unidos en 1982.

TIN THƯ Avenues

TÍN CHỈ 3 **Một Lần Bị Bão**

Bài Hát Về Thời Tiết

Trong tín chỉ này, chúng ta sẽ học về thời tiết.

1. Hát một bài ca, hay kể một câu chuyện về thời tiết quý vị học được lúc còn bé.
2. Bảo con của quý vị vẽ một bức tranh trên mặt sau tờ giấy này để nhắc nhở em nhớ về ý nghĩa của bài thơ hay bài hát.
3. Giúp con của quý vị viết lại bài thơ hay bài hát. Nhắc em mang lời ghi chú và bức tranh vào lớp học.

Chúng Ta Đang Đọc Những Gì

"Cơn Gió Xoáy"

Trong chuyện này, một gia đình sống sót qua một cơn trốt xoáy.

"Cơn Bão Lớn"

Bài bào tin tức này nói về một cơn bão dữ đã quét ngang qua Hoa Kỳ vào năm 1982.

气象歌

在这一单元里我们学习天气现象。

1. 讲述你孩提时学到的有关天气的诗、歌或谚语。
2. 让你的孩子在这张纸的背面画出这首诗、这首歌的大意。
3. 帮助你的孩子写下这首诗或这首歌的歌词。提醒你的孩子上课时带上写的笔记和画的图画。

读书目录

《龙卷风》

这是一个家庭经历龙卷风劫后余生的故事。

《暴风骤雨》

这篇新闻报道讲述一场1982年横扫美国的巨大的暴风雨。

Avenues 뉴스레터

유닛 3

폭풍우 이야기

날씨와 관련된 노래

이 유닛에서는 날씨에 대하여 배웁니다.

1. 부모가 어렸을 때 배운 시, 노래, 속담들을 얘기해 주십시오.
2. 얘기해 준 시나 노래와 관련된 그림을 이 페이지 뒷면에 그리라고 하십시오.
3. 시나 노래를 적는 데 도와주십시오. 적은 것과 그림을 클래스에 갖고 가라고 하십시오.

우리가 읽고있는 책들

"회오리 바람"

한 가족이 토네이도를 경험한다.

"태풍"

이 뉴스는 1982년 미국을 휩쓸었던 태풍을 보도한다.

Kwvtxhiaj Txog Huabcua

Nyob rau tshoojntawv no, peb yuav kawm txog huabcua.

1. Qhia rau tus menyuam ib zaj pajhuam, kwvtxhiaj, los sis lus txog tej huabcua uas koj tau kawm txog thaum koj tseem yau.
2. Hais kom koj tus menyuam kos ib daim duab rau daim nplooj ntawv no sab nrauv kom pab nws nco tau tias zaj lus pajhuam los sis zaj kwvtxhiaj txhais li cas.
3. Pab koj tus menyuam sau zaj lus pajhuam los sis zaj kwvtxhiaj tseg. Hais kom nws nqa zaj lus thiab daim duab tuaj tom nws chav tsev kawmntawv.

Tej Peb Nyeem Txog

"Lub Khaubzigcua"
Hauv zaj lus no, mas tham txog tsevneeg khiav dim kob nagxob nagcua loj loj uas muaj khaubzigcua nrog.

"Kob Nagxob Nagcua Loj Loj"
Tsab ntawv xovxwm piav txog kob nagxob nagcua loj loj uas tshuab ntsawj thoob plaws thooj av U.S. thaum xyoo 1982.

BILTEN Avenues

Chante sou Tan an

Nan leson sa a, nou pral etidye fenomèn tan an.

1. Pataje yon pwezi, yon chante, oubyen yon pwovèb ou te aprann lè ou te timoun.
2. Fè pitit ou a desinen yon imaj sou do fèy sa a pou li ka sonje kisa pwezi oubyen chante sa a vle di.
3. Ede pitit ou a ekri pwezi oubyen chante a. Fè li sonje pote nòt li pran yo ak desen an nan klas la.

Kisa Nap Li

"Toubiyon"

Nan istwa sa a, yon fanmi te rive chape yon toubiyon.

"Gwo Tanpèt Lan"

Atik sa a rakonte kijan yon gwo tanpèt te bale peyi Etazini nan lane 1982.

Avenues NEWSLETTER

UNIT 4 **Watery World**

Tales of the Sea

In this unit, we will learn about the ocean and underwater creatures.

1. Share with your child a story about a sea creature you heard when you were growing up. When did you first learn the tale?
2. Have your child draw a picture on the back of this page to remind him or her about the story.
3. Have your child take notes about the story. Remind your child to bring the notes and picture to class.

What We're Reading

"The Secret Footprints"
This legend from the Dominican Republic tells the story of a tribe that lives underwater.

"Hello, Fish!"
This photo essay tells about many creatures that live in a coral reef.

Avenues 教育通讯

第四单元 | 水的世界

大海的故事

我们将在这一单元里介绍海洋和水下动物。

1. 和你的孩子共享一个你小时候听说的有关海洋动物的故事。你什么时候第一次听说这个故事的?
2. 让孩子在这张纸的背面画一幅能提醒他或她这个故事的图画。
3. 帮助你的孩子写出有关这一故事的笔记。提醒你的孩子上课时带上写的笔记和画的图画。

读书目录

《神秘的脚印》

这是一个来自多米尼加共和国的民间传说，讲述了在水下居住的部落的故事。

《你好啊，鱼!》

这一组照片描述了不少栖息在珊瑚礁中的水下动物。

Avenues 뉴스레터

바다의 이야기

이 유닛에서는 바다와 해저 동물들에 대하여 배웁니다.

1. 부모가 어릴 때 들은 바다 속의 동물에 대하여 들려주십시오. 언제 이 이야기를 처음 들었나요?
2. 이 페이지 뒷면에 그 이야기와 관련된 그림을 그리라고 하십시오.
3. 그 이야기에 대하여 적으라고 하십시오. 적은 것과 그림을 클래스에 갖고 가라고 하십시오.

우리가 읽고 있는 책들

"비밀의 발자욱"
물속에서 사는 원주민에 관한 도미니칸 공화국의 전설

"헬로 피시"
산호 안에서 사는 많은 해양 동물들을 소개하는 사진 에세이.

Avenues TSAB XOVXWM

TSHOOJNTAWV 4 — **Lub Ntiajteb Ntub Ntsuav**

Dabneeg Txog Hiavtxwv

Nyob rau tshoojntawv no, peb yuav kawm txog dej hiavtxwv thiab cov tsiaj nyob hauv dej.

1. Piav rau koj tus menyuam mloog txog ib tug tsiaj hauv hiavtxwv uas koj tau hnov thaum koj tseem pib hlob tuaj. Koj paub txog zaj dabneeg no thaum twg?
2. Hais kom koj tus menyuam kos ib daim duab rau daim nplooj ntawv sab nrauv kom pab nws nco tau zaj dabneeg.
3. Hais kom koj tus menyuam muab zaj lus sau tseg. Nco ntsoov hais kom koj tus menyuam nqa zaj lus thiab daim duab tuaj tom nws chav tsev kawmntawv.

Tej Peb Nyeem Txog

"Cov Hneevtaw Zais Tseg"

Zaj dabneeg nrov nrov tuaj tebchaws Dominican Republic tuaj no mas hais txog haiv neeg uas nyob hauv qab deg.

"Hello, Ntse!"

Daim duab thiab cov lus sau muab los no mas qhia txog ntau hom tsiaj nyob rau ntawm cov txha paj zeb (coral reef) hauv dej.

Ti Istwa sou Lanmè a

Nan leson sa a, nou pral etidye fenomèn lanmè ak bèt kap viv anba dlo.

1. Aprann pitit ou a yon istwa sou yon bèt ki viv nan lanmè ke ou te aprann lè ou te timoun. Kote ou te aprann ti istwa sa a?
2. Fè pitit ou desinen yon imaj sou do fèy sa a pou li ka sonje istwa a.
3. Mande pitit ou pran nòt sou istwa wa. Fè li sonje pou li pote nòt li pran yo ak desen nan klas la.

Kisa Nap Li

"Mak Pye Sekrè"

Lejann sa a ki soti nan peyi Repiblik Dominikèn pale nou sou yon tribi moun ki te viv anba dlo lanmè.

"Alo, Pwason!"

Ansanm foto sa yo montre nou tout kreyati kap viv nan yon resif.

A Little Piece of Home

In this unit, we will read about immigrants to the U.S. who brought a little piece of home with them.

1. Help your child interview family members or friends who have a special object to remind them of their home country.
2. Have your child write the name of the person, a description of the object, and what it means to the person. Remind your child to bring the notes to class.

What We're Reading

"The Lotus Seed"

In this story, an immigrant from Vietnam brings a lotus seed with her to remind her of her home country.

"Where We Come From"

In their own words, six young immigrants tell about life in the United States.

Un pedacito de allá

En esta unidad, leeremos sobre inmigrantes a los Estados Unidos que traen consigo un pedacito de su país.

1. Ayude a su hijo o hija a entrevistar a familiares o amigos que guardan un objeto especial como recuerdo de su país de origen.
2. Pida a su hijo o hija que apunte el nombre de la persona, la descripción del objeto, y el significado que tiene el objeto para esa persona. Recuérdele a su hijo o hija que debe traer los apuntes a la clase.

Estamos leyendo...

"La semilla de loto"

En este cuento, una inmigrante de Vietnam se trae consigo una semilla de loto como recuerdo de su tierra.

"De dónde somos"

En sus propias palabras, seis jóvenes inmigrantes cuentan sobre su vida en los Estados Unidos.

TIN THƯ Avenues

TÍN CHỈ 5 **Những Ràng Buộc Văn Hoá**

Một Chút Quê Hương

Trong tín chỉ này, chúng ta sẽ đọc về những di dân đến Hoa Kỳ mang theo một chút quê hương của họ.

1. Giúp con của quý vị phỏng vấn những người thân trong gia đình hay bạn bè nào có một kỷ vật đặc biệt nhắc họ nhớ đến quê hương.
2. Bảo con của quý vị viết tên của người đó, lời mô tả về kỷ vật, và vật này có ý nghĩa gì đối với người đó. Nhắc em mang lời ghi chú này vào lớp học.

Chúng Ta Đang Đọc Những Gì

"Hột Sen"

Trong chuyện này, một di dân từ nước Việt Nam mang theo một hột sen bên mình để nhắc nhở cô nhớ về quê hương xứ sở của cô.

"Chúng Ta Từ Đâu Đến"

Bằng ngôn ngữ riêng của mình, sáu người di dân trẻ tuổi kể về đời sống tại Hoa Kỳ.

Avenues 教育通讯

一小片故土

我们在这一单元里介绍在美国安家立业的移民们，带来的代表他们故土的纪念物。

1. 帮助你的孩子采访一位拥有怀念故土的特殊纪念品的亲友。
2. 让你的孩子写下这位亲友的名字、纪念品的形状和对主人的意义。提醒你的孩子上课时带上写下的笔记。

读书目录

《荷花种子》

在这个故事里，一位越南移民带来了荷花种子，以寄托她对家乡的思念。

《我们来自何方》

六位年青的移民分别用他们自己的语言，讲述了来美国后的生活。

Avenues 뉴스레터

고향의 한 조각

이 유닛에서는 고향의 한 조각을 갖고 미국에 이민 온 사람들에 대한 이야기를 읽습니다.

1. 이민 올 때 고향에서 특별한 물건을 갖고 온 가족이나 친구를 만나 대화할 수 있도록 자녀를 도와주세요.
2. 그 사람의 이름을 적고, 어떤 물건인지 그리고 그 사람에게 어떤 의미가 있는지 적으라고 하십시오. 적은 것을 클래스에 갖고 가라고 하십시오.

우리가 읽고 있는 책들

"연꽃 씨"

월남에서 온 이민자가 고향의 향기를 맞기 위하여 연꽃 씨를 갖고 이민 왔다.

"우리는 어디서 왔는가"

6명의 젊은 이민자들이 미국에서 생활을 직접 말한다.

Ib Nyuag Qhov Txog Kuv Tej Vajtsev

Nyob rau tshoojntawv no, peb yuav nyeem txog cov neeg tsiv teb tsaws chaw tuaj nyob rau U.S. uas nqa ib nyuag qhov khoom txog lawv tej vajtsev tuaj nrog lawv.

1. Pab koj tus menyuam tham nrog koj tsevneeg los sis tej phoojywg uas nqa ib yam khoom dab tsi tsiv nrog lawv tuaj es lawv thiaj tau saib ua ib qho chaw tshua txog lawv tej vajtsev.
2. Hais koj tus menyuam sau tus neeg ntawd lub npe, sau qhia saib yam khoom zoo li cas, thiab muaj nqi li cas rau tus neeg ntawd. Hais kom koj tus menyuam nqa zaj lus tuaj tom nws chav tsev kawmntawv.

Tej Peb Nyeem Txog

"Lub Noob Paj Doj-Npuas"

Hauv zaj lus no, tus neeg tsiv teb tsaws chaw tuaj nyab-laj tebchaws tuaj tau nqa lub noob paj doj-npuas tuaj cia tau saib ua ib qho chaw tshua txog nws lub tebchaws.

"Peb Tuaj Qhov Twg Tuaj"

Cov menyuam hluas 6 leej uas tsiv teb tsaws chaw tuaj nyob rau tebchaws United States, lawv tus kheej kiag piav txog lawv lub neej nyob rau tebchaws no.

Yon Ti Souvni Lakay

Nan leson sa a, nou pral li sou imigran Etazini ki te vini ak yon ti souvni de peyi lakay yo.

1. Ede pitit ou a fè entèvyou ak moun nan fanmi ni oubyen ak zanmi ki te vini ak yon objè espesyal ki fè yo sonje lakay yo.
2. Mande pitit ou a pou li ekri non moun sa a, deskripsyon souvni an epi ki enpòtans li genyen pou mèt li. Fè li sonje pote nòt li pran yo nan klas la.

Kisa Nap Li

"Grenn Lotis la"

Nan istwa sa a, yon imigran peyi Vyètnam vini ak yon grenn lotis pou li ka sonje peyi li.

"Kote Nou Moun"

Sis jenn moun ap pale, nan jan pa yo, sou lavi nan peyi Etazini.

Avenues NEWSLETTER

UNIT 6

This State of Mine

A Coin of Our Own

In this unit, we will learn about state history.

1. Look at coins with your child. Talk about the images you see on them.
2. Work with your child to draw a coin to honor your family or your home country. Have your child draw a picture of it on the back of the page.
3. Have your child describe the coin here. Remind your child to bring the description and picture to class.

What We're Reading

"A Quarter's Worth of Fame"

In this interview, a Massachusetts boy explains how he won a contest to design the state's quarter.

"The Tree That Would Not Die"

An oak tree tells the state history of Texas from its point of view.

Nuestra propia moneda

En esta unidad, aprenderemos la historia de algunos estados de Estados Unidos.

1. Con su hijo o hija, examine varias monedas. Comenten sobre las imágenes que hay en ellas.
2. Trabaje con su hijo o hija para dibujar una moneda que represente su familia o país de origen. Pida a su hijo o hija que dibuje el diseño de la moneda al otro lado de esta hoja.
3. Pida a su hijo o hija que describa la moneda aquí. Recuérdele que debe traer esta hoja a la clase.

Estamos leyendo..

"Una moneda famosa"

En esta entrevista, un chico de Massachusetts explica cómo ganó un concurso para diseñar una moneda del estado.

"El árbol que no moría"

Un roble cuenta la historia de Texas desde su punto de vista.

TIN THƯ Avenues

TÍN CHỈ 6 Tiểu Bang Này Của Tôi

Đồng Tiền Kim Loại Của Riêng Chúng Ta

Trong tín chỉ này, chúng ta học về lịch sử của tiểu bang.

1. Hãy cùng con của quý vị nhìn vào đồng tiền kim loại. Nói về những hình ảnh quý vị thấy trên đó.
2. Cùng với con của quý vị vẽ một đồng tiền kim loại để vinh danh gia đình hay tổ quốc của quý vị. Bảo con của quý vị vẽ một bức tranh trên mặt sau của trang giấy này.
3. Bảo con của quý vị viết lời mô tả đồng tiền kim loại vào đây. Nhắc con của quý vị mang bài mô tả này và bức tranh vào lớp học.

Chúng Ta Đang Đọc Những Gì

"Đồng Hai Mươi Lăm Xu Danh Dự"

Trong cuộc phỏng vấn này, một cậu bé ở tiểu bang Massachusetts giải thích việc cậu thắng giải thi vẽ kiểu đồng hai mươi lăm xu của tiểu bang như thế nào.

"Cây Không Bao Giờ Chết"

Một cây sồi kể về lịch sử của tiểu bang Texas trên quan điểm của nó.

Avenues 教育通讯

我们自己的硬币

在这一单元里，我们将学习本州的历史。

1. 和你的孩子一起研究不同的硬币，并讨论硬币上的图案。
2. 和你的孩子一起设计一枚家庭或故乡的纪念硬币。让你的孩子在这张纸的背面画出这个硬币的图案。
3. 让你的孩子解释一下设计的图案。提醒你的孩子上课时带上图案的立意和画的图案。

读书目录

《二十五美分获得盛名》

这是一篇对麻萨诸塞州一名男孩的采访。这个男孩在设计本州二十五美分硬币的竞标中获胜。

《长生不老的树》

一棵橡树以它的独特立场叙述了德克萨斯州的历史。

Avenues 뉴스레터

우리 자신만의 동전

이 유닛에서는 주 역사에 대하여 배웁니다.

1. 자녀와 함께 동전을 살펴보세요. 동전에 새겨진 그림들에 대하여 애기하세요.
2. 자녀와 함께 동전을 그리면서 가족과 고국에 경의를 표하십시오. 이 페이지 뒷면에 그 이야기와 관련된 그림을 그리라고 하십시오.
3. 어떤 동전인지 설명하라고 하십시오. 적은 것과 그림을 클래스에 갖고 가라고 하십시오.

우리가 읽고 있는 책들

"25센트 가치의 명성"

매사스추세츠에 사는 한 소년은 자신이 어떻게 주 정부 쿼터 동전 디자인 컨테스트에 당선되었는가를 설명한다.

"죽지 않는 나무"

오크 나무가 자신의 입장에서 텍사스의 역사를 얘기한다.

Lub Npib Uas Yog Peb Lub

Nyob rau tshoojntawv no, peb yuav kawm txog cov xeev tej keebkwm.

1. Nrog koj tus menyuam neb muab npib coj los xyuas. Tham txog cov duab pom nyob rau ntawm cov npib.
2. Nrog koj tus menyuam neb kos ib lub npib muaj duab hawm txog nej tsevneeg los sis txog nej lub tebchaws. Hais kom koj tus menyuam kos daim duab rau daim nplooj ntawv no sab nrauv.
3. Hais kom koj tus menyuam sau piav txog lub npib rau qhov no. Nco ntsoov hais kom nws nqa tej lus nws sau piav thiab daim duab tuaj tom nws chav tsev kawmntawv.

Tej Peb Nyeem Txog

"Muaj Moo Phim Lub Quarter"

Nyob rau zaj lus xam-phaj no, tus menyuam tub nyob Massachusetts piav tias nws ua li cas es tus qauv nws kos ua lub npib quarter rau nws lub xeev thiaj raug xaiv ua lub yeej.

"Rob Ntoo Uas Yeej Tsis Txawj Tuag"

Rob ntoo Oak tree qhia txog lub xeev Texas lub keebkwm, raws li Texas hais.

BILTEN Avenues

Pyès Monnen Pa Ou

Nan leson sa a, nou pral etidye istwa leta a.

1. Gade kèk pyès monnen ak pitit ou a. Diskite sou imaj ou wè ki grave sou yo a.
2. Ansanm ak pitit ou, eseye desine yon pyès monnen an lonnè fanmi ou oubyen peyi lakay ou. Mande pitit ou a desinen li nan do fèy sa a.
3. Mande pitit ou a pou li dekri pyès monnen sa a. Fè li sonje pote deskripsyon ak foto sa a nan klas la. Nan leson sa a, nou pral etidye istwa leta a.

Kisa Nap Li

"Yon Pyès Goud Eka Pote Laglwa"

Nan entèvyou sa a, yon ti gason nan leta Masachousèt rakonte kijan li genyen nan yon konkou pou desin pyès goud eka leta a.

"Pye Bwa ki Pap Janm Mouri A"

Yon pye chenn ap rakonte istwa leta Tegzas jan li wè l la.

Avenues NEWSLETTER

UNIT 7 **What's It Worth?**

Sayings About Money

In this unit, we will read about money and its value.

1. Here is one saying about money: "A penny saved is a penny earned." What sayings about money do you know? Share them with your child.
2. Choose one saying. Talk about what the saying means.
3. Help your child write down the saying. Remind your child to bring the notes to class.

What We're Reading

"My Rows and Piles of Coins"

In this story, a young boy saves his hard-earned coins to buy a bicycle.

"Money"

This social studies article gives information about the history and importance of money.

BOLETÍN Avenues

UNIDAD 7 **¿Cuánto vale?**

Dichos acerca del dinero

En esta unidad, leeremos sobre el dinero y su valor.

1. Éste es un dicho sobre el dinero: "Un centavo ahorrado es un centavo ganado". ¿Qué otros dichos sobre el dinero conoce usted? Compártalos con su hija o hijo.
2. Escojan un dicho. Comenten su significado.
3. Ayude a su hijo o hija a escribir el dicho. Recuérdele que debe traer sus apuntes a la clase.

Estamos leyendo...

"Pilas de monedas"

En este cuento, un niño ahorra sus monedas para comprar una bicicleta.

"Dinero"

Este artículo de ciencias sociales habla de la historia e importancia del dinero.

Avenues 뉴스레터

돈에 대한 이야기

이 유닛에서는 돈과 그 가치에 대하여 배웁니다.

1. 돈과 관련된 속담: **"**1전을 절약하면 곧 1전을 버는 거다.**"** 돈과 관련된 속담을 알고 계시나요? 자녀에게 말해 주세요.
2. 그 중에 하나를 선택하세요. 그 속담의 의미에 대하여 말하세요.
3. 그 속담을 쓰라고 하십시오.

우리가 읽고 있는 책들

"나의 동전 꾸러미"
한 소년이 열심히 모은 동전으로 자전거를 산다.

"돈"
돈의 역사와 중요성을 설명하는 소설 스터디.

Tej Lus Hais Txog Nyiaj

Nyob rau tshoojntawv no, peb yuav nyeem txog nyiaj thiab nyiaj tus nqi.

1. Nov yog ib lo lus pivtxwv txog nyiaj: "Ib lub npib liab tseg, yog ib lub npib liab khwv tau." Puas muaj tej lo lus pivtxwv txog nyiaj uas koj paub? Piav qhia rau koj tus menyuam.
2. Xaiv ib lo lus pivtxwv. Es piav saib lo lus yog txhais li cas.
3. Pab koj tus menyuam muab lo lus sau tseg. Hais kom tus menyuam nqa zaj lus thiab daim duab tuaj tom nws chav tsev kawmntawv.

Tej Peb Nyeem Txog

"Kuv Pawg Raj Npib"

Hauv zaj lus no, tus menyuam tub tau siv zog khwv nyiaj tseg nws cov npib coj mus yuav ib lub lub-tees.

"Nyiaj"

Zaj kev txujci txog kev haumxeeb tau qhia rau peb paub txog nyiaj lub keebkwm thiab txog tias nyiaj no tseemceeb npaum cas.

Pwovèb Sou Lajan

Nan leson sa a, nou pral li sou zafè lajan ak valè li.

1. Men yon pwovèb sou zafè lajan: "Yon senk kòb sere se yon senk kòb ki rapòte w." Ki pwovèb ou konnen sou zafè lajan? Pataje yo ak pitit ou.
2. Chwazi yon pwovèb. Eksplike sa li vle di.
3. Ede pitit ou a ekri pwovèb la. Fè li sonje pote nòt li te pran yo a nan klas la.

Kisa Nap Li

"Tout Ti Pil Pyès Monnen Mwen Yo"

Nan istwa sa a, yon jenn gason ap sere tout ti pyès monnen li yo pou li sa achte yon bisiklèt.

"Lajan"

Atik syans sosyal sa a pale sou istwa ak enpòtans lajan.

Avenues NEWSLETTER

UNIT 8 **Rocky Tales**

A Stone for Each Month

In this unit, we will learn about rocks.

1. In the U.S, there are stones that represent each month of the year. They are called birthstones. Look at this list. Does it match what you know? If not, work with your child to list stones you know.
2. Talk about why people value certain rocks.
3. Ask your child to draw his or her birthstone on the back of this page. Have him or her add the name of the stone and the month. Remind your child to bring this paper to class.

What We're Reading

"Call Me Ahnighito"
In this story, a meteorite tells about its journey from Greenland to a New York museum.

"The Life Story of a Rock"
This science article tells how rocks are formed and why they are important.

Birthstones in the United States

January: garnet	April: diamond	July: ruby	October: opal
February: amethyst	May: emerald	August: peridot	November: topaz
March: aquamarine	June: pearl	September: sapphire	December: turquoise

BOLETÍN Avenues

La piedra del mes

En esta unidad, aprenderemos sobre las piedras.

1. En los Estados Unidos, hay piedras preciosas que corresponden a cada mes. Mire esta lista. ¿Son las mismas piedras que usted conoce? Si no, trabaje con su hijo o hija para anotar las piedras del mes que usted conoce.
2. Comenten por qué algunas piedras son más valiosas que otras.
3. Pida a su hijo o hija que, al otro lado de esta hoja, dibuje su propia piedra del mes. Dígale que anote el nombre de la piedra y el mes. Recuérdele que debe traer esta hoja a la clase.

Estamos leyendo...

"Me llamo Ahnighito"
Un meteorito describe su viaje desde Groenlandia hasta un museo en Nueva York.

"La historia de una roca"
Este artículo de ciencias explica cómo se forman las piedras y por qué son importantes.

Piedras del mes en Estados Unidos

enero: granate	abril: diamante	julio: rubí	octubre: ópalo
febrero: amatista	mayo: esmeralda	agosto: peridoto	noviembre: topacio
marzo: aguamarina	junio: perla	septiembre: zafiro	diciembre: turquesa

TIN THƯ Avenues

TÍN CHỈ 8 — **Chuyện Cổ Về Đá**

Một Hòn Đá Cho Mỗi Tháng

Trong tín chỉ này, chúng ta sẽ học về đá.

1. Tại Hoa Kỳ, Có những loại đá tượng trưng cho mỗi tháng trong năm. Người ta gọi chúng là đá tháng sinh (birthstones). Hãy nhìn vào bảng liệt kê bên dưới. Xem có trúng với những gì quý vị biết không. Nếu không, cùng với con của quý vị liệt kê những loại đá quý vị biết.
2. Thảo luận tại sao con người quý báu một số loại đá nào đó mà thôi.
3. Bảo con của quý vị vẽ loại đá tháng sanh của em trên mặt sau tờ giấy này. Bảo em viết thêm tên của đá và tháng tương ứng. Nhắc em mang giấy này vào lớp học.

Chúng Ta Đang Đọc Những Gì

"Gọi Tôi Là Ahnighito"

Trong chuyện này, một thiên thạch kể về cuộc hành trình của nó từ Greenland đến một viện bảo tàng ở New York.

"Chuyện Đời Của Đá"

Bài báo khoa học này nói về đá được hình thành như thế nào và tại sao chúng được xem là quan trọng.

Birthstones Tại Hoa Kỳ

Tháng Giêng: ngọc hồng lựu	Tháng Tư: kim cương	Tháng Bảy: hồng ngọc	Tháng Mười: ngọc mắt mèo
Tháng Hai: ngọc tím	Tháng Năm: ngọc xanh lục	Tháng Tám: ngọc xanh vàng	Tháng Mười Một: ngọc vàng
Tháng Ba: ngọc xanh biển	Tháng Sáu: ngọc trai	Tháng Chín: ngọc bích	Tháng Mười Hai: ngọc lam

每月一石

我们在这一单元里将学习有关岩石的知识。

1. 在美国，不同的石头代表着一年不同的月份，它们叫作生辰石头。看看下面的列表。其中说的和你知道的一样吗？如果不一样，和你的孩子一起列出你所知道的石头。
2. 讨论人们为什么赋予石头以特殊的价值。
3. 让孩子在这张纸的背面画出他或她的生辰石头，并且写出石头的名字和相应的月份。提醒你的孩子上课时带上这张纸。

读书目录

《称我阿尼黑陶》

在这个故事里，一颗陨星叙述了自己从格陵兰 (Greenland) 到纽约 (New York) 博物馆的旅程。

《一块岩石的生平》

这篇科技文章阐述了岩石是如何形成的以及它的重要性。

美 国 的 生 辰 石

一月：石榴石	四月：钻石	七月：红宝石	十月：蛋白石
二月：紫水晶	五月：翡翠	八月：橄榄石	十一月：黄玉石
三月：绿玉	六月：珍珠	九月：兰宝石	十二月：绿宝石

Avenues 뉴스레터

탄생석

이 유닛에서는 보석에 대하여 배웁니다.

1. 미국에서는 매 월을 상징하는 보석이 있습니다. 탄생석이라고 부릅니다. 이 목록을 한 번 보세요. 여러분이 알고 있는 것과 같나요? 같지 않다면, 자녀와 함께 여러분이 알고 있는 보석을 열거해 보세요.

2. 사람들은 왜 특정 돌맹이를 보석으로 여기는지 생각해 보세요.

3. 이 페이지 뒷면에 자신의 탄생석을 그리라고 하십시오. 보석의 이름을 해당 월을 추가하라고 하십시오. 적은 것을 클래스에 갖고 가라고 하십시오.

우리가 읽고 있는 책들

"나를 아니히토라고 부르세요"
운석이 경험한 그린랜드에서 뉴욕 박물관까지의 여행.

"돌맹이의 인생 이야기"
돌맹이가 어떻게 형성되며 그 중요성을 설명한다.

미국의 탄생석

1월: 석류석	4월: 다이아몬드	7월: 루비	10월: 오팔
2월: 자수정	5월: 에머랄드	8월: 페리도트	11월: 토파즈
3월: 아콰마린	6월: 진주	9월: 사파이어	12월: 터키옥

Avenues TSAB XOVXWM

TSHOOJNTAWV 8 — **Dabneeg Txog Pobzeb**

Ib Lub Pobzeb Rau Ib Lub Hli

Nyob rau tshoojntawv no, peb yuav kawm txog pobzeb.

1. Nyob rau hauv U.S. mas nws muaj cov pobzeb sawvcev rau txhua txhua lub hli. Luag hu lawv ua birthstones. Xyuas ntawm cov lus hauv qab no. Nws puas zoo tib yam li cov koj paub? Yog tsis zoo, ces nrog koj tus menyuam sau cov npe pobzeb koj paub rau.
2. Tham txog tias ua cas neeg thiaj muab pobzeb saib muaj nqis heev.
3. Hais kom koj tus menyuam kos ib daim duab txog nws lub pobzeb birthstone rau daim nplooj ntawv no sab nrauv. Hais kom nws sau lub npe pobzeb thiab lub hli rau lub pobzeb ntawd. Nco ntsoov hais kom koj tus menyuam nqa daim ntawv tuaj tom nws chav tsev kawmntawv.

Tej Peb Nyeem Txog

"Hu Kuv Hu Ua Ahnighito"

Hauv zaj lus no, lub hnubqub meteorite piav txog thaum nws mus Greenland rau lub tsev museum nyob New York.

"Zaj Lus Piav Txog Lub Pobzeb Lub Neej"

Tsab ntawv science no qhia txog tias ua cas thiaj li muaj pobzeb thiab vim li cas cov pobzeb thiaj tseemceeb heev.

Cov Hli Npe Tis Nrog Rau Pobzeb Nyob Rau Hauv United States

Lub Ib Hli Ntuj: pobzeb garnet
Lub Ob Hli Ntuj: pobzeb amethyst
Lub Peb Hli Ntuj: pobzeb aquamarine
Lub Plaub Hli Ntuj: pobzeb diamond
Lub Tsib Hli Ntuj: pobzeb emerald
Lub Rau Hli Ntuj: pobzeb pearl
Lub Xya Hli Ntuj: pobzeb ruby
Lub Yim Hli Ntuj: pobzeb peridot
Lub Cuaj Hli Ntuj: pobzeb sapphire
Lub Kaum Hli Ntuj: pobzeb opal
Lub Kaum Ib Hli Ntuj: pobzeb topaz
Lub Kaum Ob Hli Ntuj: pobzeb turquoise

Yon ti Pyè Presie Pou Chak Mwa

Nan leson sa a, nou pral etidye pyè presie.

1. Ozetazini, genyen yon pyè presie pou chak mwa nan ane a. Yo rele yo "birthstones" (pyè presie ki reprezante mwa ou fèt). Gade lis sa a byen. Eske ou rekonnèt yo? Sinon, eseye ak pitit ou wa pou ekri pyè presie ou konnen.
2. Pale sak fè sèten moun pito sèten pyè.
3. Mande pitit ou a pou li desinen pyè presiez pa li lan do fèy sa a. Fè li make non ak mwa pyè an. Fè li sonje pote fèy la nan klas la.

Kisa Nap Li

"Rele Mwen Ahnighito"

Nan istwa sa a, yon meteyò ap rakonte vwayaj li soti "Grinnlan" rive nan yon mize Nouyòk.

"Istwa Lavi Yon Pyè"

Atik syantifik sa a montre kijan wòch fèt ak sak fè yo gen enpòtans.

Pyè Presie Ozetazini

Janvye: wouj grena	Avril: dyaman	Jiyè: wouj vif	Oktòb: opal
Fevriye: ametis	Me: vèt enmwòd	Out: peridòt	Novanm: topaz
Mas: ble vèt	Jen: pèl	Septanm: ble syèl	Desanm: tikwaz